LENA NACHMANOVICH BUSCH
MINSK 1872 – NEW BRUNSWICK 1946

y Tree

Nachmanovich
David Leib + Sarah

Lena
b. 1872 – 11·3·46

Elizabeth + Julius Medwin 1000-1970 1006-1941
Rose + Lev 3·17·11
Florence Shulman Cynnie + Louis Boyer
Jean Fox 6·11·12   12·12·09

—ois + Jeanette Hoffman
—5·11·06   3·12·98

Sarah + Emmett Jopkins
3·1·09   9·13·06 – 11·25·64

Henry + Kathleen Miller
12·23·10   9·4·14 – 7·10·79

Florence + Carl Grossman
9·15·14 – 10·8·81   11·4·12

—lin Ronald Bertram
4   10·18·38   4·28·41

Margot
3·12·38

Elliott
3·22·43

Mark
11·24·42

Lillian
Norma Bertha
9·12·14

Leonard
1·28·47

Jay
3·2·46

Laura
4·16·49

—ra Carol Linda
—rlin Rubenstein Rosenbaum
—57   4·16·39   6·9·42

Marshall
Suttin
12·6·33

Wendy
Tarlow
2·11·44

Frankie
Liebermann
11·5·45

Lois
Livingston
10·21·46

Donna
Selett
11·22·48

Arthur
Lifshutz
10·28·47

—z Julie
7·9·
Matthew Roger
60   10·31·68
Gregory
—62 6·22·71
Emily
5·15·75
—id
—rick

David
Emmett
9·2·72
Andrew
3·14·76

Joanne
Little
3·12·53
Alex
3·14·86
Dana
7·29·89

Caroline
9·20·68
Johanna
5·14·71

Donna
née Lewis
12·1·51
Robin
9·17·74
Jonathan
1·5·77

Brandon Weir
12·9·75
Joey
Kenny
Reuben
Spencer
10·22·80
Ashley
9·30·82

Sammy
9·13·80
Marla
5·24·85

Diana
1·31·67
John
Campbell
11·4·61
Alison
8·19·69
Erica
2·10·7
Alyson
Sutton
11·2·90

Gwen
10·25·61

Scott S. Packman
5·10·68
Griffin
96
m. 3·9·96

—rew Rebecca Debbie
—5·65 Maline
—aget to 6·26·91
—d Pine
—ned 1·8·6
3·92
—a Lee
12·14·94
—rmin Eli
3·6·97

Hilary
11·22
Michael
Levey
Michael
3·23·95
Erik Lewis
11·6·95

Theodore + Lauren Kelleher
2·9·64

Emily + John Stachowiak 11·1·92
1965-1995
Michael Matkul 11·16·85
Paul
4·16·67
Jonathan Vogel
6·13·70
m. 9·6·97

The Jews of New Jersey

The Jews
of
New Jersey

A Pictorial History

PATRICIA M. ARD
AND
MICHAEL AARON ROCKLAND

12/4/01

For Bob Wilder

From the authors!

Michael Aaron Rockland

Patricia Ard

RUTGERS UNIVERSITY PRESS
New Brunswick, New Jersey

Publication of this book was assisted by a grant from the New Jersey Historical Commission, a division of Cultural Affairs in the Department of State.

Library of Congress Cataloging-in-Publication Data

Ard, Patricia M., 1955–
    The Jews of New Jersey : a pictorial history / Patricia M. Ard and Michael
      Aaron Rockland.
      p. cm.
    ISBN 0-8135-3012-1 (alk. paper)
      1. Jews—New Jersey—History. 2. Jews—New Jersey—History—Pictorial
    works. 3. New Jersey—Ethnic relations. I. Rockland, Michael Aaron.
    II. Title.

    F145.J5.A74 2001
    974.9'004924—dc21

                                            2001019837

British Cataloging-in-Publication information is available from the British Library.

Manufactured in the United States of America

For our children, Kathleen Sarah Ard Rockland
and Joshua Sean Ard Rockland

Contents

Preface

WHEN RUTGERS UNIVERSITY PRESS suggested we create this book, we were skeptical it could be done. The topic seemed too broad. Which Jews in which towns and cities? we wondered. What time period? We knew that one book could not begin to grapple with the totality of New Jersey Jewish life or, if it did, would offer its readers a poor smorgasbord rather than a good meal.

We have tried to avoid these traps. We have focused, in the book's eleven chapters, on those aspects of New Jersey Jewish life that are, in our judgment, especially significant and concerning which we were able to collect good pictures and good stories. We wanted the book to be as interesting graphically as historically. Some fine stories we heard could not be documented with pictures. Some wonderful pictures had to be discarded because we could not ascertain important facts about them. The book is in no way a definitive history of the Jews of New Jersey. Everyone who reads it will, no doubt, take some exception to what it emphasizes and what it leaves out.

In our choices of material we have concentrated on the past, assuming that contemporary pictures and stories may already be familiar to the reader and of less interest thematically and graphically. We also wished to make some small contribution to the graphic arts and to share with the reader not only antique styles of dress but of photography: how people were posed by photographers and how these people who stare out at us wished to be seen.

Thomas Carlyle wrote, "In a sense, all men are historians," and this is certainly true of the women and men who took these pictures and who appear in them. If we look at these pictures more than cursorily, they tell us much about who these people were, how they lived, and what their ideas and aspirations were.

In concentrating on the past we also wished to focus on New Jersey Jews before they joined mainstream culture, before they became relatively accepted—a time when they were less assimilated. We wanted to concentrate on a time when the Italian word "ghetto" (originally the neighborhood in which Jews were confined in Venice) still described, to a certain extent, Jewish rather than African-American and Hispanic neighborhoods and when there was no uncertainty as to whether Jews were a "minority." The 1950s seemed a convenient breakpoint between when Jews were still very much "the other" and when they became increasingly assimilated into mainstream New Jersey life, and the great majority of the pictures in this book and the stories accompanying them precede that time.

We also decided that this would be a book not about famous New Jersey Jews but about the texture of everyday life for New Jersey's 460,000 Jews and their ancestors. We were not interested in celebrating this Jewish scientist, that Jewish poet, or constructing yet another book full of revelations that such-and-such a movie star or politician or athlete is/was Jewish. We believe the Jewish community has become sufficiently self-confident and mature, and that America has become sufficiently accepting of Jews, that it is no longer necessary to engage in this form of Jewish public relations. On the rare occasions when famous Jews appear in these pages it is not in celebration of their careers but to illustrate a point about the evolution of New Jersey Jewish life.

Collecting these photographs and stories has been an adventure in itself, often involving equal parts luck and detective work. Sometimes we heard of important pictures by word of mouth, and often people

Jewish tradesmen in Paterson. This photograph, circa 1930, shows David Zakim, housepainter, and Max Goldberg, plumber, each with the tools of his trade. *Jewish Historical Society of North Jersey*

with pictures heard of us the same way. More than once people entrusted us with crumbling family photo albums that had to be re-assembled afterward.

Sometimes we came across vast caches of wonderful photographs, and their owners went out of their way to share them with us. Other times we labored for weeks to obtain what turned out to be a single photograph of dubious utility. However these photographs were obtained, in the course of doing so we have come to know many wonderful people and made new friends.

Especially helpful have been the various New Jersey Jewish newspapers, which, for no charge, advertised our search for photographs. We have also been helped immensely by county and local historical societies and by various town, county, and university archives. Most helpful of all have been the five Jewish historical societies of New Jersey, which are struggling institutions in need of, and immensely worthy of, support.

We wish to acknowledge the following institutions and people who generously helped us with their time, stories, and their photographs. We consider them true partners in the creation of this book: Gloria Weiss Allen, Morristown; Karen Anolick, Morris Township; Ron Becker, Director of Special Collections and University Archives, Rutgers University Libraries; Dick Bergman, Princeton; Ruth Schreibstein Bogutz, Tri-County Jewish Historical Society, Camden; David Brandt, Cherry Hill; Sidney Chonowski, Randolph; Vivienne Cohen, Springfield; Shirley Cook, Hackensack; John Corcoran, Gloucester City; David Cowen, Monroe Township; Flora Buchbinder Cowen, Edison; Charles Cummings, Newark Public Library; Cheryl Dennison, Mendham; Gertrude Dubrovsky, Princeton; Nat Dunetz, Jewish Historical Society of MetroWest; Donna Ezor, *The Jewish News,* Whippany; Charles Feldman, Teaneck; Gilbert and Lynn Finkel, Morristown; Hans Fisher, Rutgers University; Alise Ford, Mendham; Sheldon Freidenreich, Edison; Jill and Paul Gallner, Jewish Federation of Greater Monmouth Country; Brigitte Goldstein, Highland Park; Helene Grynberg, Old Bridge; Charlotte Kruman, Rumson; Bunny Kuiken, American Labor Museum, Haledon; Ruth B. Mandel, Eagleton Institute of Politics, Rutgers University; Phyllis Mankoff, Temple B'nai Jeshurun, Short Hills; Keith Miller, Deal; the Morristown and Morris Township Public Library; Jerry Nathans, Jewish Historical Society of North Jersey; Corinne Nifoussi, Piscataway; David Nussbaum, Jewish Federation of Greater Monmouth County; Vera Nussenbaum, Old Bridge; the Art Gallery of Ontario (Toronto); Jayne O'Connor, Office of the Governor of New Jersey, Trenton; Donna Parris, East Hanover; Ruth Patt, Jewish Historical Society of Central Jersey; Princeton University Library; Ari and Marilyn Rabinowitz, Highland Park; Nathan Reiss, Highland Park; Rabbi Don Rosoff, Temple B'nai Or, Morristown; Paul Schopp, Camden County Historical Society; Shari Segel, Museum of Jewish Heritage, New York; Joanne Seiter, Camden County Historical Society; Joseph Settanni, Jewish Historical Society of MetroWest; Yvonne Skaggs, Princeton; Maureen Smyth, Princeton Historical Society; the late Paul Stellhorn, Newark Public Library; Gail Stern, Princeton Historical Society; Sol Stetin, Paterson; Marlene and Robert Stevens, Short Hills; Rabbi Israel Teitelbaum, Rabbinical College of America, Morristown; Marie Varner, New Milford; Edna Wechsler, Monroe Township; Rachel Weintraub, Jewish Historical Society of Central New Jersey; Mel Woda, Ocean Township; Abraham Zuckerman, Hillside; and Orvill Zuckerman, Jewish Historical Society of Greater Trenton.

Many people at Rutgers University Press were instrumental in the creation of this book, but we want especially to single out Marlie Wasserman, David Myers, Marilyn Campbell, and Patricia Politi who were full partners of ours in conceiving this book and who gave us constant and ready support in our work.

Patricia M. Ard

Michael Aaron Rockland

Morristown, New Jersey

January 2001 Shevat 5761

The Jews of New Jersey

Immigration and
Early Jewish Settlers

THE HISTORY OF THE JEWS in New Jersey follows a trajectory similar to the histories of Jews in other locales in the United States, especially those urban areas where sizable Jewish populations congregated. Jews came ashore in the New World along with the earliest European settlers. Sephardic Jews who had been expelled from Spain and Portugal traveled to Brazil; and when the Portuguese brought the Inquisition there, they sailed in 1654 for New York, where Peter Stuyvesant attempted unsuccessfully to deny them admission. By 1698, the merchant Aaron Louzada and his family, believed to be the earliest Jews to settle in New Jersey, had built a home in Bound Brook. Sephardic Jews were followed by successive waves of German Jews in the 1840s and Eastern European Jews beginning in the 1880s.

These migrations often resulted from hostile and at times deadly conditions and events that Jews experienced abroad. Barnet Silberman emigrated from Minsk, Russia, and became a builder in Woodbine, a Jewish farming community in Cape May County. "Here in America it's safe. You can play out of doors," he told his children, suggesting how, in the United States, Jews could live a public life as Jews, no longer driven indoors to worship or live in secret.

Jews from the eighteenth century who chose to settle in New

Samuel and Rachel Sarah Marcus with sons Abraham (*l.*) and Joseph (*r.*) on arrival in America, 1896. They settled in the New Brunswick area.
Jewish Historical Society of Central New Jersey

Barnet Silberman, born in Minsk, Russia, in 1862, was one of the chief carpenter-builders of housing in Woodbine. Here he is shown with his children. His great-granddaughter, Marie Varner, was told by her grandmother, Marie, standing at left, that one of her father's favorite expressions was, "Here in America it's safe. You can play out of doors."
Marie Varner

The Fisher family, photographed shortly after arriving in the United States from Kiev, Ukraine, circa 1907: Nathan, Max, Bess, Pearl, and Ida. The family eventually settled in Bridgeton.
Paul Gallner

David Naar (1800–1880), mayor of Elizabeth, aide to President James K. Polk, and holder of countless public offices, was one of the state's early Jewish residents. Emigrating from the Virgin Islands, Naar worked in the Democratic party and as a journalist and supporter of public education in Trenton, which made him one of the state's most prominent Jews in the nineteenth century.
Newark Public Library

Jersey benefited from its early embrace of the secular liberalism of Revolutionary-era American thought. And New Jersey was the first state to adopt the Bill of Rights. The brief bursts of religious antagonism mentioned in early histories of the state generally concern Protestant antagonism to "Papists." By 1844 the state constitution had specifically abolished religious qualifications for public activities such as holding office. These laws of inclusion made New Jersey more hospitable than many other states for Jews.

Two early Jews who took advantage of New Jersey's inclusive sensibility were Daniel Nunez and David Naar. In the 1720s Nunez became town clerk and tax collector for Piscataway and municipal justice in Middlesex County, probably the first Jew to hold public office in the United States. Naar settled in Elizabeth in 1835 and eventually served as its mayor.

Portrait of Sarah Marks Stockton by Thomas Sully, 1847. In 1845 John Potter Stockton, a descendant of a signer of the Declaration of Independence, married Sarah, a Jew from New Orleans. The marriage caused a scandal in the Protestant-dominated community of wealthy Princetonians. Although Sarah attended services at the Episcopal church in town, her diary reveals the abuse she was subjected to because of her religious background.

Samuel Judah (1799–1869) was the first Jew to graduate from Rutgers University, called Queens College at the time. He was one of five graduates in the class of 1816 and went on to become a prominent lawyer and legislator in the new state of Indiana. Judah's parents and their nine children were part of a small second wave of Jews into the New Brunswick area. His father, Bernard, had trained as a doctor under Samuel Bard, the personal physician to George Washington.
Jewish Historical Society of Central Jersey

Jews mingled with the life of the state, but slowly. Asher Levy is one of the few Jewish names listed as a New Jersey soldier in the Revolutionary War. In the mid-nineteenth century Sarah Marks, a Jew from New Orleans, married John Potter Stockton, a member of an old Princeton family. Sarah was never accepted into the life of the town and complained bitterly about the bias she experienced even when she began worshipping in the Episcopal church. However, down the road in New Brunswick's Queens College, later renamed Rutgers University, Samuel Judah became the college's first Jewish graduate in 1816, seemingly without incident.

Newspaper boys, mostly Jewish, take a break from their work on State and Broad Streets, Trenton, 1908. Selling papers was a common first job for immigrant boys.
Jewish Historical Society of Greater Trenton

The treasured Naturalization Certificate of Benjamin Friedman, a Russian immigrant who settled in Passaic.
North Jersey Jewish Historical Society

One of Samuel Asbell's two grocery stores on Broadway in Trenton, circa 1917. This is probably the store at 811 Broadway.
Tri-County Jewish Historical Society Collection at the Camden County Historical Society

Rabbi Louis Segal and family: wife Esther, sons Sam and Nathan, daughter Sadie, Camden, circa 1910. Early synagogues in New Jersey generally functioned without rabbis until they began to arrive from Europe in larger numbers. Rabbi Segal served at the Liberty Street Synagogue in Camden from 1910 to 1925, one of eight synagogues that once called Camden home. Today, no functioning synagogues exist in Camden; most have relocated to Cherry Hill.
Tri-County Jewish Historical Society Collection at the Camden County Historical Society

Jews and other immigrants wait for the ferry to the Central New Jersey Railroad Station in Jersey City, New Jersey, early 1900s. The railroad took immigrants to New Jersey towns and points west. Although many Jews rode the ferry from Ellis Island to New York, the fact that two-thirds of the more than twelve million people who passed through Ellis Island between 1892 and 1954 took the ferry to New Jersey suggests that, contrary to popular belief, many immigrants, Jewish and otherwise, first landed in New Jersey rather than Manhattan.
Ellis Island Immigration Museum

Sephardic and German Jews arrived in such relatively small numbers that they were largely ignored or generally accepted, but when streams of Eastern European Jews began arriving late in the nineteenth century, Jews found themselves increasingly segregated in "Jewtowns." Such anti-Semitism was nevertheless more tolerable than the death threats, pogroms, and forced conscriptions Jews had faced abroad. Indeed, unlike some fellow immigrants, such as many Italians, Jews came to the United States to stay, largely because they had no place to which to return. Thus, until 1924—when the United States began to look differently at all immigrants and, out of fear of their influence, drastically reduced the numbers accepted—Jewish immigrants flowed into the United States.

Certain traditional religious practices of these immigrants were gradually moderated in order to better fit into American society and a business world that often required working six or seven days a week, including the Sabbath. The separation of men and women during religious services and other traditional practices contrasted with the more casual and egalitarian atmosphere outside the synagogue's doors. And when Rabbi Isaac Mayer Wise of Cincinnati founded American Reform Judaism, he signaled that immigrant Jews needed to create a Judaism that was different from what it had been in Europe and to become Americanized.

Most Jewish immigrants to New Jersey settled in the urban corridor from Middlesex to Bergen County in the north. They were accustomed to living in cities, coming from the crowded conditions of European ghettos and shtetls, and they had worked in the Old Country as factory workers and storekeepers. Women had often been employed outside the home in Europe, a pattern that continued in America. "Cobblers' wives must make the thread. . . . Tailors' wives must sit up late," went a Yiddish folksong, confirming the reality of the double shift of household drudgery and exhausting jobs so many women performed. But that double shift gave Jewish women a taste for independence and a desire for education, which may account for why Jewish women have been so prominent in the contemporary feminist movement.

Jewish immigrants are harder to track than other ethnic groups because Jews came from not one but many different countries. Although there were numerous entry ports for immigrants, the majority before 1954 came to the United States through Ellis Island, which was recently determined by the United States Supreme Court to be primarily in New Jersey, and is, besides, much closer to the Garden State than to New York. Thus, while many Jewish immigrants headed for Manhattan's fabled Lower East Side, many others took the ferry from Ellis Island to the Central New Jersey Railroad Station, which still stands in Liberty State Park. Here they boarded trains for towns in New Jersey or points west. Of those who chose to stay in New Jersey, many headed to Newark to begin life in America.

Newark

A Community Flourishes

NEWARK WAS INCORPORATED in 1836, just in time to receive the German Jewish immigrants who pioneered so much of its commerce and industry. Later, Eastern European Jews, escaping from pogroms, discriminatory taxes, and legal restrictions on education and employment, swelled the city's population.

Worship and informational meetings took place in private homes until there were sufficient funds to build a synagogue and bring a rabbi to America. The first Newark congregation, B'nai Jeshurun, was founded shortly before mid-century; only Paterson's synagogue of the same name preceded it in New Jersey. With new synagogues in a new

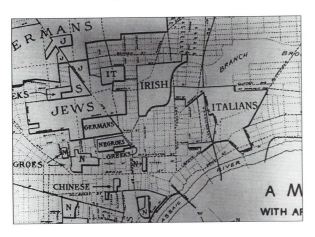

A 1911 ethnic map suggests a pre-assimilation world, as well as the variety of immigrant cultures providing workers for Newark's industry. Many groups congregated, or felt forced to congregate, in neighborhoods where they could be with people who spoke their language and/or understood their customs. Jews, of course, came from different countries and often found other Jews almost as unfamiliar as non-Jews.
Jewish Historical Society of MetroWest

Shoppers on Prince Street, the commercial center of the Jewish section of turn-of-the-century Newark. Clothing and Jewish food specialties of all types were available here. The noise of carriages rumbling over paving blocks and merchants hawking wares from pushcarts is a scene remembered by many first-generation Jewish residents of Newark.
Newark Public Library

country, however, came changes. Once governed by rabbis, scripture, and halacha (Jewish law), immigrants began to adopt new traditions. Many synagogues, for example, initially conducted services in Yiddish, but the spirit of independence engendered by the New World would inspire Jews to shape uniquely American forms of Judaism.

In Newark, many immigrants supported synagogues according to their country of origin. For example, Polish immigrants attended B'nai Abraham, while Russian Jews attended Anshe Russia. There seemed to be a synagogue for every Jewish sensibility, and the history of Jewish Newark is filled with ideological disputes that led to divisions into new congregations. Eventually, there would be as many as fifty synagogues in Newark, providing a range of essential services to their congregants—worship, nursery care for the children of working parents, book lending, family counseling, and translation assistance. The diversity and magnitude of services represented the Jewish belief that aid to others in

The Armm brothers. The Armm family opened the first kosher restaurant in Newark, on Broome Street.
Jewish Historical Society of MetroWest

this life is of primary importance. The Talmud dictates that a good deed or charity—*tsedaka*—is equal to all other religious tenets combined.

Many of the talents that Jews brought from abroad found ready outlet in the growing industrial and commercial city that was Newark, a city of immigrants. The first Jewish resident was Louis Trier, a tanner. Soon tailors and peddlers were also abundant, moving from street selling to small shops, congregating in an area of Newark which eventually became the Third or Central Ward. Much of early Jewish life centered around Prince Street and Springfield Avenue. By 1948 some 58,000 Jews lived in Newark, accounting for 12 percent of its population. But the Central Ward was only the first of an upwardly mobile progression of Jewish enclaves in Newark. Jews would soon move to Clinton Hill and then to the Weequahic and Forest Hill areas. Not surprisingly, when upward mobility continued to the suburbs, nearby towns such as Belleville, Hillside, and the Oranges were primary choices.

A scene on Mulberry Street in Newark, circa 1915, gives a sense of the ferocious rush of business and personal trade conducted as pedestrians attempt to negotiate the horse and buggy, motorized car, and trolley traffic converging around them. Newark was often called the "Workshop of the Nation," with many Jews among its workers.
Jewish Historical Society of MetroWest

Interior of Weingarten's Corset Factory on High Street, circa 1905. Many Jewish immigrant women worked outside the home, using skills they brought from Europe and earning both much needed income and a certain independence.
Jewish Historical Society of MetroWest

A class at the Plaut Memorial Hebrew Free School on Prince Street, 1900. The principal, Meyer Hood, and a teacher, Miss Siedler, are on the right. The school was started in 1888 by rabbis of three Newark temples—B'nai Jeshurun, Oheb Shalom, and B'nai Abraham—to serve the children of the unaffiliated. It was part of the institution-building that occurred at a rapid pace in Newark to keep up with the expanding Jewish population.
Jewish Historical Society of MetroWest

Although earlier immigrant groups tended to feel superior to later arrivals, the charity of well-established Jews toward the community as a whole was a hallmark of Jewish life in Newark. In the second half of the nineteenth century and beginning of the twentieth, many Jewish residents of the Third Ward and the other Jewish sections of Newark needed such charity. Conditions in the wooden tenements and multi-family houses were crowded and cold in winter, hot in summer. Many apartments had no bathrooms, so public baths around the city were visited once a week. Conditions in Newark's innumerable factories were usually miserable. In concert with Jewish workers in nearby Paterson, labor unions, many of whose leaders were Jews, became another force of uplift for impoverished immigrants. Of course, not all Jews entered reputable professions. Abner "Longy" Zwillman of Newark was one of the chief gangsters of the early twentieth century. "I had to get money somehow," he explained. "I got it—bootlegging."

An outing of Newark's No Name Club. The odd name was picked to "arouse the inquisitiveness of non-members . . . and thus make them anxious to apply for admission." Later it was renamed the Progress Club; its members socialized, sponsored events of Jewish interest, and regularly discussed business and political issues.
Jewish Historical Society of MetroWest

For most Jews, however, poverty increased their desire to succeed through education. Temples such as B'nai Jeshurun provided day schools and Hebrew schools when public education was not yet freely available. The Plaut Memorial Hebrew Free School and the Talmud Torah of Newark, both founded in the late nineteenth century, were important sources of Jewish education. Jewish social clubs such as the No Name Club, an early club for businessmen to meet and make connections, as well as the numerous Zionist clubs that appeared in the 1920s, were a key ingredient of Jewish community life. Major Jewish philanthropic societies appeared in Newark, continuing a tradition of providing aid to the needy.

The centrality of family life to the Jewish community was reflected in these charities. The Friendly Sisters was organized in 1852 to help families in need, and the Hebrew Benevolent and Orphan Asylum Society began its work shortly after. Philanthropy and community building

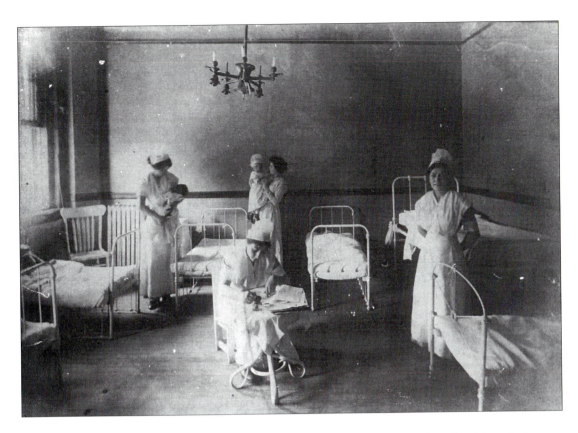

The nursery of Beth Israel Hospital in 1916. Like colleges that limited the number of Jewish students, many hospitals prior to World War II had quotas for the number of Jewish doctors they would hire or to whom they would grant professional privileges. Beth Israel was created in 1902 in response to this anti-Semitism, and to serve the needs of the Jewish immigrant community, among others. Eventually it would move to Lyons Avenue and expand to become a prestigious institution, well known for several specialty areas of treatment and, of course, open to all.
Jewish Historical Society of MetroWest

The Newark YMCA basketball team of 1919. Milton Schlosser, seated in the middle, was a third-generation German-American Jew. As his membership on the YMCA's team suggests, German-American Jews were well integrated into American culture when Russian and other East European Jews began arriving in large numbers in the 1880s. Schlosser married Essie Yawitz, a Russian Jew, and their families considered the union a mixed marriage. Some German-American Jews called themselves "Hebrew" instead of Jewish, believing that the former had a better connotation, referring as it did to an ancient language and people. Russian Jews often wondered if German-American Jews were Jews at all.
Alise Schlosser Ford

This poster was designed by Louis V. Aronson for the building fund drive for the High Street YM-YWHA, 1920.
Jewish Historical Society of MetroWest

such as that sponsored by the department store businessman Louis Bamberger, his sister Caroline Bamberger Fuld, and many others in the early decades of the twentieth century dispersed Jewish culture and community life throughout the state. Although anti-Semitism was prominent in the years leading up to World War II, Jewish philanthropists as well as Jews in the arts and sciences contributed to Jewish acceptance. Newark's "golden age" of the 1920s through the 1940s saw the building of an enlarged Beth Israel Hospital and cultural institutions such as the famed High Street YM-YWHA and the Newark Museum; all these institutions benefited from the generosity of Louis Bamberger. After World War II, the Jewish Family Service Association of Essex County assisted Jewish families in Europe by helping to bring them to the Newark area to start a new life.

The High Street YM-YWHA became a cultural center of Jewish activity for every member of the family. Opened in 1924, the Y responded to the fact that many Jews in Newark were not affiliated with a temple; some young Jews lived in tenements and had no other opportunities for recreation. The Y's first director, Dr. Aaron G. Robinson, stated that the Y would be "the town hall of the Jewish Community."
Jewish Historical Society of MetroWest

The Lewitt family illustrates the immigrant experience of Jews in Newark. In 1885, sixteen-year-old Martha and her eighteen-year-old husband, Julius, left Russia and came to Newark with their newborn son, Max. They stayed briefly with a Jewish family before establishing a butcher shop and a home of their own. Julius and Martha later sponsored other members of their family to come to the United States. Julius's brother, Ellis, came to Newark and both raised their families there. Julius and Martha had eight children, three sons and five daughters, who lived and worked in Newark, owned several businesses, raised families, and contributed to the solidarity of the Jewish community. The third Newark generation of Lewitts also married and lived in Newark but then joined the exodus to the suburbs.

With the dispersal of Jews to the suburbs, Newark as a great center of Jewish life disappeared. In the most suburban state in the nation, Jewish life now flourishes in a more decentralized way than it did when Newark was its focus. What was once the Jewish Federation of Newark

Julius and Martha Lewitt, with son Max, four, and daughter Fannie, two, in front of Julius and Martha's grocery/butcher shop in Newark, 1889. The "e" was later dropped from the family name.
Jewish Historical Society of MetroWest, Nat Dunetz Collection

Julius and Martha's daughter, Fannie Lewitt Bernstein, December 1918. Fannie is shown working at the Bergen Street Pharmacy owned by her brother Max Lewitt. During World War I, Fannie worked at the three Newark pharmacies of her brothers to keep the businesses going.
Jewish Historical Society of MetroWest, Nat Dunetz Collection

May 21, 1919, Newark Parade of War Veterans. Fannie Lewitt Bernstein's husband, David Bernstein, is third from left.
Jewish Historical Society of MetroWest, Nat Dunetz Collection

The July 2, 1921, opening of Lewitt's department drugstore at Market and Washington Streets, Newark. Using the occasion of the Carpentier-Dempsey fight, the store owners arranged to have the fight professionally announced at their store. The owners described the scene as follows: "A crowd estimated at over thirty thousand people lined the curbs and walks of both Market and Washington Streets, and the initial details of six mounted policemen weren't sufficient to hold them in check and had to be reinforced by several more sent from headquarters." Dempsey won the fight.
Jewish Historical Society of MetroWest, Nat Dunetz Collection

George Lewitt, son of Julius and Martha, holding his niece, Julia (or Jewel) Bernstein, Newark, 1921.
Jewish Historical Society of MetroWest, Nat Dunetz Collection

now is found on a highway near Morristown and is known not as the "Newark Federation" or even the "Essex County Federation," but simply as "MetroWest." MetroWest is an interesting term, suggestive of a sentimental need to remain attached to urban origins while recognizing how much Newark's Jews, like early pioneers, have headed west. While the Whippany-based MetroWest serves Essex, Warren, Morris, Sussex, and parts of Union, Somerset, and Hudson counties, its large facility serves many Jews from other northern New Jersey counties as well as non-Jews. A less cohesive, more heterogeneous Jewish community needs a community center, and MetroWest supplies that need.

Wedding of Edna Jacobson and Walter Wechsler in Congregation Ahavas Sholom in Newark, 1940. Edna Wechsler's parents were among the founders of the congregation, which built its temple on Broadway in 1921. Besides the Mount Sinai congregation, which holds services in an apartment complex, the synagogue is the last one functioning in Newark today.
Edna Wechsler

Congregation B'nai Zion, now closed, and, as shown, damaged by vandals. Newark's many synagogues were either abandoned or adapted for other uses after Jews, who had been migrating to other New Jersey towns, accelerated that process in the 1940s and 1950s, and especially after the Newark riots of 1967.
Jewish Historical Society of MetroWest

B'NAI JESHURUN:
ONE CONGREGATION'S STORY

From Newark to Short Hills, from Orthodox to Reform, from worship in a congregant's home to a succession of locations, Congregation B'nai Jeshrun has seen many changes in its nearly 160-year history.

B'nai Jeshurun, meaning "Children of the Upright," was founded in 1848 as an Orthodox synagogue. Three of the five signers of the incorporation papers were brothers: Abraham, Solomon, and Isaac Newman. Abraham's grandson, Jacob Newman, a lawyer who practiced in Newark, was the congregation's president when the temple celebrated its 100th anniversary in 1948. Earlier, in 1881, the congregation became the first in New Jersey to join the Reform movement.

A Jew from England, Isaac Cohen, provided the congregation's first worship space in his home. Initially without a rabbi, the congregation rapidly outgrew Cohen's home and rented a succession of spaces. Eventually, it erected its own building on Washington Street

Temple B'nai Jeshurun's Washington Street building, 1868–1915.
Temple B'nai Jeshurun

in 1858. In 1868 it moved to larger quarters on Washington Street and in 1915 to a new building on High Street.

The High Street synagogue served the congregation from 1915 to 1968. Pews in this synagogue were sold to members as a way to finance the building. But as more congregants moved to the suburbs, B'nai Jeshurun established an alternate, suburban location in the 1950s, using a renovated home on Center Street in South Orange for certain functions. Thus, its transition to the suburbs took place gradually.

In 1968, the current, modern temple in Short Hills was dedicated. B'nai Jeshurun's several sites are emblematic of the history of the Jews of Newark and their movement through

Interior of Temple B'nai Jeshurun on Sukkot, at the High Street location.
Temple B'nai Jeshurun

Temple B'nai Jeshurun, Short Hills, its location since 1968.
Temple B'nai Jeshurun

and eventually out of the city to the surrounding suburbs. Currently serving over 1,200 families, the Short Hills location maintains a sense of the temple's past in photos and artifacts from prior locations scattered throughout the building. Descendants of the Newman family still belong to the congregation. Wherever it has been situated, from Isaac Cohen's home in Newark to its current quarters in Short Hills, B'nai Jeshurun has retained the spirit of its original Newark-based founders.

CHAPTER

3

Paterson, Trenton, and Camden

MAJOR URBAN CONCENTRATIONS of Jews in New Jersey, outside Newark could be found throughout the state. As in Newark, only tiny pockets of Jews remain in Paterson, Trenton, and Camden, typically the elderly. In most cases synagogues have been abandoned, demolished, or renovated for other purposes. Where the magnificent Barnert Temple once stood in Paterson, for example, there is now a White Castle. And what was once the thriving Jewish Federa-

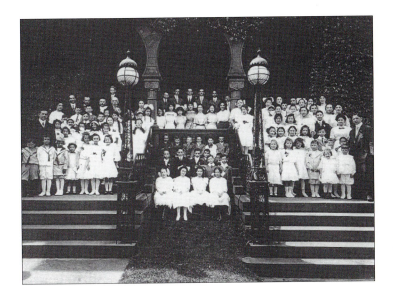

Children's classes on the steps of Barnert Temple in Paterson (now the site of a White Castle) in 1911. *Jewish Historical Society of North Jersey*

tion of Trenton is now the Jewish Federation of Princeton, Mercer County, and Bucks County—ample evidence not only of how few Jews still live in Trenton but of how far this particular Jewish community has spread out, even crossing the Delaware to neighboring Pennsylvania. But today's changing geography of Jewish settlement does not negate the vitality and charm of New Jersey's Jewish urban life of yesteryear. The Lower East Side in Manhattan, so celebrated in books such as Irving Howe's *World of Our Fathers* and movies such as *Hester Street,* had its parallels in several of New Jersey's urban areas.

Paterson

When one thinks of Paterson, the word "labor" immediately comes to mind. During the Revolutionary War period, Alexander Hamilton stood by the Great Falls of the Passaic and, impressed by its potential as a source of power, declared that Paterson would become America's first great manufacturing center. That it did. In the mid-nineteenth century Paterson was the national center of locomotive manufacturing, while

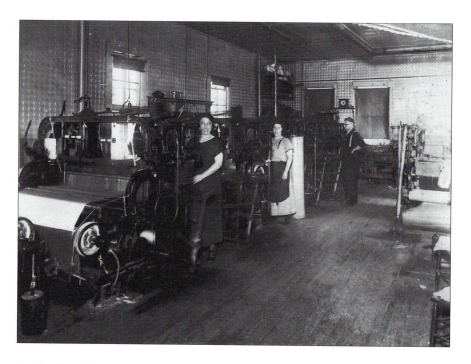

Jewish silk workers at their looms in one of Paterson's 292 silk factories, circa 1900. *American Labor Museum, Botto House*

A house that silk built. This turn-of-the-century twenty-room French Renaissance-style residence was built on Paterson's East Side by Charles Simon, a silk magnate and great-grandfather of William E. Simon, secretary of the treasury under Presidents Richard Nixon and Gerald Ford. Later, it became an Orthodox Jewish synagogue (as pictured here). Today, it houses a Catholic order.
Jewish Historical Society of North Jersey

later in that century and into the early twentieth silk became its key industry. Especially prominent in the latter endeavor were Jews—many from Bialystok and Lodz, Poland, key Eastern European textile centers—who had migrated with their skills in needle trades intact.

Jews were prominent not only as silk manufacturers but as laborers and labor leaders, and the Paterson silk strike of 1913 was one of the key events in the development of the American labor movement. Twenty-four thousand workers went out on what proved to be a seven-month strike. The American Labor Museum is installed in Haledon, just outside Paterson, in the national landmark Botto House, where strikers congregated for rallies because they were prohibited from doing so in Paterson itself.

Jews in Paterson were, of course, active in activities other than labor and manufacturing, such as the professions and commerce. Paterson's most prominent Jewish citizen was Nathan Barnert, who migrated to the United States in 1849 as a poor eleven-year-old and made a fortune

Children of Paterson silk strikers, most of them Jewish, in 1913. With their parents out of work for many months and with little or no family income, these children and others were sent to friends and relatives in New York.
Jewish Historical Society of North Jersey

The headquarters of the silk-worker's union (circa 1930) at the corner of Washington and Broadway, above a bustling street scene below.
Jewish Historical Society of North Jersey

Sol Stetin (left), a Jewish immigrant from Poland, has been prominent in the American labor movement his entire life, notably as founder of the Amalgamated Clothing and Textile Worker's Union. This photo was taken on Tyler Street in Paterson, circa 1927, with Stetin's friend Ben Miller. Stetin was also the founder of the American Labor Museum in Haledon, just outside Paterson. A character in the Academy Award–winning film *Norma Rae* is based on him. At age ninety, he still lives in Paterson.
Sol Stetin

THE WORKMEN'S CIRCLE CHORUS
ORGANIZED PATS'ONS FEB. 1923

Because of intense labor-organizing activity in the area, Paterson's Jews were especially involved in socially oriented causes in the days before welfare, social security, or unemployment insurance. The Workmen's Circle, which combined democratic socialism and the secular teaching of Jewish values in what it called "shulas" (schools), had, in its heyday in the 1920s, fourteen branches and 84,000 members in New Jersey. It also sponsored cultural groups such as the Paterson chorus, pictured here in 1923.
Jewish Historical Society of North Jersey

Dr. Morris Joelson and son in his horse-drawn buggy in front of his Paterson office, circa 1915.
Jewish Historical Society of North Jersey

Several Jewish shops are in evidence in this 1920 photograph of Main Street near its intersection with Van Houten in Paterson.
Jewish Historical Society of North Jersey

A 1915 photograph of the interior of Federbush's, a general store located on Broadway in Paterson, which sold appliances and supplies of all kinds.
Jewish Historical Society of North Jersey

Nathan Barnert, longtime mayor of Paterson, reading a speech of appreciation for the new statue of him unveiled in 1925.
Jewish Historical Society of North Jersey

The YMHA float after a parade, circa 1918. "What We Have Done," the float proclaims, advertising the Y's many charitable activities. The soldier with the missing leg would seem to be Exhibit A.
Jewish Historical Society of North Jersey

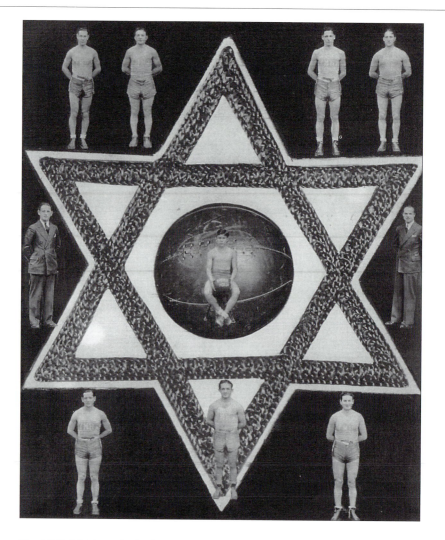

The 1935–36 YMHA basketball team.
Jewish Historical Society of North Jersey

in various endeavors, including gold mining in California. He was elected mayor of Paterson at age forty-five and served two terms. In his later years, he devoted himself to philanthropy, founding and supporting a variety of Jewish institutions including temples, schools, a hospital, and an old-age home, several of which still exist. In 1925 a statue of Barnet was erected in front of Paterson City Hall.

Among the institutions Barnert supported was the YMHA. Generally, Jews were either excluded from YMCAs or preferred to have their own Ys, where not only Jewish athleticism but Jewish culture might flourish. Paterson's Y was first located on Broadway and was extremely active, not only in Jewish life but in Paterson as a whole.

Trenton

The center of the Jewish neighborhood of Trenton was located where the Hughes Justice Complex stands today. Earlier, it had been an Irish neighborhood, later an African-American one.

Like many Jewish neighborhoods in other New Jersey cities, Trenton's was often referred to as "Jewtown." However harsh this may sound today, at the time it was not necessarily considered offensive. One elderly Jewish Trentonian remembers a friendly Irish bus driver who, approaching the neighborhood, would cheerfully say, "All off for the Holy Land," or "All off for Jewtown."

Just as the relative offensiveness of words evolves over time, so do ethnic characteristics associated with foods. For example, pizza today has lost many of its specifically Italian associations and become a prominent American food. Similarly, bagels, which were once a strictly Jewish

Neighborhoods of the poor and oppressed have traditionally given rise to prizefighters. Boxing—where one earns a living getting beaten up—has long been a ticket out of poverty. The Irish were the great fighters of the late nineteenth century, the Italians of the mid-twentieth century, African Americans and Hispanics more recently. Jews were prominent in American prizefighting in the 1910s and 1920s. Here Michael Schlossberg, a light heavyweight in the 1920s, stands in front of Ben's Delicatessen on Lamberton Street with Market Street in the background. *Jewish Historical Society of Greater Trenton*

Samuel Kohn (left, with cigar) in front of Kohn's bakery at Market and Broad, circa 1920. An unidentified worker stands on the right, with Kohn's daughter Frieda in the doorway. Note the challahs in the window. *Jewish Historical Society of Greater Trenton*

Kohn's bakery with daughter Mayo on a Sunday in the 1920s. Jewish shop owners closed on the Sabbath and found it a hardship to also close on Sunday as required by blue laws. Often Jewish merchants were summoned to the police station on Monday to pay a two-dollar fine for having stayed open on Sunday. Samuel Kohn worked out a compromise with the chief of police. If he hung the curtain in his window on Sundays, signaling to gentile customers that he was closed, Jewish customers could enter the bakery through the rear and purchase their pumpernickel and rye breads and bagels.
Jewish Historical Society of Greater Trenton

Another Trenton Jewish bakery, Kramer's, on Livingston Street, circa 1947. This photograph was taken in the middle of the night, when bagels were baked. Ozzie Zuckerman, now president of the Jewish Historical Society of Greater Trenton, owned a delicatessen at that time and would go by Kramer's at 3 A.M. to pick up some three hundred bagels every night.
Jewish Historical Society of Greater Trenton

The New York Delicatessen on East Front Street on March 22, 1922. From left, Ted Kalish, Harry Kalish, and Barney Schulman.
Jewish Historical Society of Greater Trenton

Louis Kupersmit in front of his candy and tobacco store on North Broad Street, circa 1920.
Jewish Historical Society of Greater Trenton

M&H Robinson's clothing store at 235 Ferry Street in 1915. Harry Robinson, in the derby hat, is third from left, with Meyer Robinson, center, along with family members and various employees.
Jewish Historical Society of Greater Trenton

Charlie Field outside his Trenton grocery store in the early 1940s, when milk came in bottles that were returned for the deposit.
Jewish Historical Society of Greater Trenton

The Moses Cleaning & Dyeing Co. on South Broad Street, circa 1935. Proprietor Ed Moses stands with his foot on the running board of one of his trucks, his employees on the left.
Jewish Historical Society of Greater Trenton

Isaac Goldberg (front, left) in Japan in 1917, where he had gone to purchase kimonos to sell in Trenton. When the Japanese factory was destroyed in an earthquake in 1923, killing most of its workers, Goldberg brought the three survivors and many of their friends and families to Trenton to work in his factory on Donnelly's Alley off Lamberton Street. Here he manufactured what he called "coolie coats," which were quite the fashion rage in America in the 1920s.
Jewish Historical Society of Greater Trenton

bakery product in Trenton and elsewhere, have become ubiquitous in America. Jews wearing yarmulkes were once referred to as "bagel-heads," yet few who buy bagels today think of them as Jewish food; indeed, many bagel store operators are not Jewish. Young people today often think of pizza and bagels as central to American cuisine and not especially ethnic at all.

In addition to being prominent in the bakery business, Jews also dominated other lines of commerce, including delicatessens, candy and tobacco stores, clothing stores, and grocery stores.

Trenton's slogan is "Trenton Makes, The World Takes," and Trenton's Jews, in addition to being shopkeepers, engaged heavily in industry and manufacturing.

ONE TRENTON FAMILY

Orvill "Ozzie" Zuckerman was a naval aviator in World War II. When he returned to his family in Trenton, he worked as a photographer for several years, learning the trade from his mother, who had photographed the Wright Brothers at Kitty Hawk. Indeed, Orvill was named after Orville Wright, but, he quips, "The doctor's pen ran out of ink so he left off the 'e.'" Today, Ozzie writes a regular column for *The Jewish News* and is the president of the Jewish Historical Society of Greater Trenton. "I'm the keeper of the flame," he says.

Ozzie Zuckerman as an airman during World War II.
Jewish Historical Society of Greater Trenton

The Zuckerman family in 1932. Ozzie Zuckerman sits in the front row, third from left.
Jewish Historical Society of Greater Trenton

The Zuckerman family in 1960, with everyone in exactly the same position as in the 1932 photograph, right down to Ozzie Zuckerman's sister (standing on left), who holds a flower in both pictures.
Jewish Historical Society of Greater Trenton

Camden

Camden, like Paterson and Trenton, has virtually no Jews today, and there are no functioning Jewish institutions. It is, therefore, difficult to imagine the former vitality of its Jewish community and the large part it played in the city's cultural life and economy. Once Camden had a vigorous economy, with RCA and Campbell's Soup as major employers.

Rabbi Naftoli N. Riff was, from the early 1920s through the late 1960s, the revered spiritual leader of Congregation Sons of Israel, often referred to as "the Eighth Street Shul" (now located in Cherry Hill).
Tri-County Jewish Historical Society Collection at the Camden County Historical Society

Rabbi Riff (second row, center) with his study class in 1944 at the Eighth Street Shul.
Tri-County Jewish Historical Society Collection at the Camden County Historical Society

The staff of Camden's Antler Baths, circa 1910, when many homes did not have bathing facilities.
Tri-County Jewish Historical Society Collection at the Camden County Historical Society

Camden B'nai Brith Community Seder - Tuesday, 1933

A community seder in 1933 at the Walt Whitman Hotel in Camden, then the city's leading hotel, located at Sixth and Cooper Streets. America's great poet Walt Whitman lived in Camden in his declining years and is buried there.
Tri-County Jewish Historical Society Collection at the Camden County Historical Society

The football team of the Jewish Community Center of Camden in the mid-1940s.
Tri-County Jewish Historical Society Collection at the Camden County Historical Society

The drum and bugle corps of the Sons of Jewish War Veterans, Post 126, Camden, in 1949. The building behind them, at 621 Kaighns Avenue, was at that time a Talmud Torah.
Tri-County Jewish Historical Society Collection at the Camden County Historical Society

A YMHA picnic of young adults from Camden in 1916 held at Blackwood, New Jersey, Gloucester Township, where one could canoe and hike or rent a bungalow.
Tri-County Jewish Historical Society Collection at the Camden County Historical Society

Louis Blum of Camden, who fought in the Spanish American War, photographed in 1898. The significance of the Stars of David on his uniform, and what, if anything, they may have had to do with his army service, is unknown.
Tri-County Jewish Historical Society Collection at the Camden County Historical Society

Jacob Furer of Camden, who fought in World War I. Furer became a lawyer and community leader after the war. The Jewish War Veterans Post of Camden, which today meets in Cherry Hill, is named for him.
Tri-County Jewish Historical Society Collection at the Camden County Historical Society

Jewish patriotism evident in the window of Jack Naden's store in Camden in 1942. Note that among those featured in his store window, at a time when the United States and Russia were allies, is Joseph Stalin (foreground center of window).
Tri-County Jewish Historical Society Collection at the Camden County Historical Society

Nurock Jewelry Store, located at 1124 Broadway in Camden, in 1902. Its gas chandeliers would soon be replaced with chandeliers equipped for both gas and electricity. Electricity was still considered too unreliable to use exclusively.
Tri-County Jewish Historical Society Collection at the Camden County Historical Society

The 1924 opening of Pinsky's Department Store, at Broadway and Spruce in Camden.
Tri-County Jewish Historical Society Collection at the Camden County Historical Society

Farmers' wagons by the hundreds lined up with their cargoes of to-matoes at the Campbell's plant. Now the company only maintains offices in the city. Camden is often held up as a case study of how much can go wrong in one city. Meanwhile, the Camden Jewish community has been virtually re-created in Cherry Hill, where it spreads out over many square miles.

Propinquity certainly is an aid to community. But affluence and the automobile have made it possible for Americans, Jews among them, to live at some distance from one another and for each family unit to be largely self-contained. Ethnic institutions suffer as a result. Characteristic of the United States, as true in suburban-oriented New Jersey as anywhere, is the lessening of the shared experiences that make for community. It can therefore be argued that while suburbs such as Cherry Hill offer much in the way of freedom, they also take away a sense of belonging.

As in the other cities, Camden's Jews were active in commerce; photographs of their stores are instructive about the taste and fashions of another time.

To the Suburbs

The New Jersey Jewish Diaspora

AS THE COMFORT and prosperity levels of Jews in New Jersey increased, a migration to the suburbs surrounding the state's major cities began. It was part of a nationwide demographic shift in the Jewish population. The mobility that universal automobile ownership has provided—not to mention the growth of Reform Judaism, which does not proscribe motoring to temple on the Sabbath—has dispersed Jewish settlement over the New Jersey countryside. Temple Sharey Tefilo was built in East Orange as early as 1874. Although Newark saw a large exodus of Jews in the 1950s and again after the riots of 1967, as early as the 1920s Jews were already leaving Newark for such nearby suburbs as Livingston and the Oranges; soon after they were leaving Camden for Cherry Hill and Trenton for Princeton. And Jews seeking escape from crowded metropolitan life had early in the twentieth century discovered Monmouth County and its breezy shore communities.

Aging has had something to do with this exodus from the cities. Older Jews seeking comfort and safety as urban problems increased have settled in retirement communities not only in Monmouth but in Miami. In 2000, with only forty members remaining, Temple Ahavath Achim in Belleville, near Newark, closed its doors and, taking its torahs and memorial plaques along, combined with the thriving congregation

Vogel Brothers Butcher Shop at 102 Nassau Street, Princeton.
Princeton Historical Society

Edith Yawitz, left, one of nine sisters, on a visit to Mount Freedom, a vibrant Jewish vacation site for many Jews from Newark early in the twentieth century.
Alise Schlosser Ford

Little Bernice Gallop Hoffman, circa 1925, in front of the Washington Hotel in Morristown. The hotel, owned by Emil and Dora Newmark, burned down about 1960. Bernice was the daughter of Lou and Laura Gallop. Laura Gallop and Dora Newmark were two of the nine Yawitz sisters. During the Depression, several of the sisters and their families had to move into the hotel.
Alise Schlosser Ford

Esse Schlosser with her children, Sidney and Elaine, circa 1931. A third child was born later. Esse, married to Milton Schlosser, was the seventh of nine daughters of Wolf and Anna Yawitz, and she and her husband lived in Morristown.
Alise Schlosser Ford

of B'nai Shalom in West Orange. "We just ran out of human beings," said Irving Berkowitz, Ahavath Achim's president. "The college crowd has moved elsewhere. We have a bigger ex-community in Florida than we do in Belleville."

A new cycle of erecting temples, Hebrew academies, and YM-YWHAs began in the suburbs, with all the attendant sports and men's and women's club activities. Temples, such as Congregation B'nai Israel in Millburn, became "safe houses" for the first Jews migrating to the suburbs who met with hostility from gentile residents. Despite anti-Semitic taunts of Jewish children at school and attempts by realtors to ghettoize prospective Jewish residents, more Jews continued to buy homes in previously Christian neighborhoods and assimilate into American culture. Milton Schlosser's explanation of his own relocation from Newark to Morristown in 1922 was the story of many a migrant to the suburbs. "I was brought here to go in business with a relative and that was rather common. . . . Someone would settle here and then some

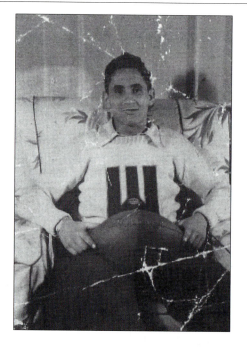

Sanford "Sandy" Pollack, circa 1945, wearing Newark's Weequahic High School letter. He played football, among other sports, at the school. Pollack was typical of many Newark natives who moved to the surrounding suburbs. He moved first to Irvington and then to West Orange, where he and his wife raised their three children. Also, like many graduates of Weequahic, he remained close to his high school friends his entire life, never truly leaving Newark behind.
Cheryl Dennison

relative and if not a relative, a close friend would . . . be sold the idea of coming out and that's the way the original Jewish population increased."

Philip Roth has written extensively on the transition of New Jersey Jews from Newark to the suburbs, most recently in *American Pastoral* (1997). Earlier, in his 1959 novella *Goodbye, Columbus,* Roth wrote: "The neighborhood has changed: the old Jews like my grandparents had struggled and died, and their offspring had struggled and prospered, and moved further and further west, towards the edge of Newark, then out of it, and up the slope of the Orange Mountains, until they had reached the crest and started down the other side, pouring into Gentile territory as the Scotch-Irish had poured through the Cumberland Gap." *Goodbye, Columbus* concerns the tension between urban and suburban values. Newark is seen as embodying traditional Jewish values, such as a commitment to learning and a cosmopolitan life, while Short Hills is seen as assimilationist, materialistic, and banal. The novella's title suggests the rejection of the latter.

One nonfictional Newark-born resident typifies the place Newark retained in the lives of those who left there in the 1950s and 1960s. Sanford "Sandy" Pollack, born in Newark in 1928, attended the almost entirely Jewish Weequahic High School and, though his family moved

Cornerstone laying ceremony for Morristown Jewish Center, March 3, 1929. Morristown's Jewish Center was typical of the many temples built by Jews who moved from Newark to surrounding suburbs and small cities in the first half of the twentieth century.
Morristown and Township Joint Public Library

Mother and daughter luncheon, May 14, 1933, Morristown Jewish Center.
Morristown Jewish Center

Rabbi Benjamin Naar, later the spiritual leader of Highland Park's Congregation Etz Ahaim, with his family in traditional Sephardic dress. The picture was taken in Salonika, Greece, before the family emigrated in 1924.
Congregation Etz Ahaim

Earliest known confirmation class, 1913 or 1914, at Anshe Emeth Memorial Temple in New Brunswick. Edith Lederer Strauss (seated), Edith Klein, Rabbi Ludwig Stern, and Toots Gorda Breitkopf.
Jewish Historical Society of Central Jersey

Paris Grocery, New Brunswick, 1919. Left to right, Albert Naar, Isaac Beja, unknown woman, Solomon Naar, Daniel Handaly. On the left window "Groceria Parisien" is written in Ladino, the language of Sephardic Jews, essentially medieval Spanish written in Hebrew letters.
Congregation Etz Ahaim

The Bruskin family of Middlesex County, circa 1905.
Jewish Historical Society of Central Jersey

Soda shop on Burnet Street in New Brunswick, circa 1930. Mrs. Harry Kotler and her son Kalman are behind the counter.
Jewish Historical Society of Central Jersey

to Irvington, remained close to his Newark friends all his life. Pollack eventually became a teacher in West Orange and was active in Jewish affairs, but, as his daughter Cheryl Dennison puts it, "He was always trying to re-create in the suburbs the life and the sense of community he knew as a boy in Newark. He had great nostalgia for Newark."

Since Jews were often restricted from local golf and country clubs, they continued to form their own institutions in the suburbs as they had in the cities. Slowly barriers fell, but as they did so did a certain degree of Jewish solidarity. To remain competitive in business, Jews found themselves remaining open on the Sabbath, especially in the difficult economic times of the 1930s. As Jews became more like everyone else, Orthodox synagogues increasingly gave way to Conservative and Reform ones. The Conservative Morristown Jewish Center was built in 1929. When a reformist trend was narrowly rejected, defeated members formed Temple B'nai Or in 1954 across town. On the other hand, Lubavitcher Hasidim brought their seminary, the Rabbinical College of

Reubin Salkin and his son Harold, June 1941, New Brunswick. Reubin Salkin was an agent for the Jewish Agricultural Society. He worked to locate farms for German Jews escaping persecution in the 1930s and 1940s. The sign on the window says "Farms Specialty." Harold was a 1941 Rutgers College graduate.
Jewish Historical Society of Central Jersey

A family portrait of the children and grandchildren of Joseph and Bella Schwartz, circa 1924, Highland Park. Joseph came to his marriage to Bella with four children from his late wife; Bella came to the marriage with two children from a prior marriage. The couple then had five children together. In a surprisingly common immigrant story, Bella's first husband had come to the United States from Russia and was supposed to send for her and the children but never did. Bella came to the United States with the children to search for her husband and found him living in Elizabeth, New Jersey, remarried and with a new family. She went to New Brunswick, briefly placed her children in an orphanage, and proceeded to get a divorce. Eventually she met Joseph and they married. Members of the fourth generation of the Schwartz family still live in Highland Park.
Marilyn Rabinowitz

Highland Park Bakery, 1927, with Moe and Helen Engelhard behind the counter. Local tutors taught Hebrew in the back room. The owners assisted customers through the Depression, liberally giving bread to those who could not afford it.
Jewish Historical Society of Central Jersey

America, from Newark to the Morristown area in 1971, suggesting the vigor of Orthodoxy in recent years, even in the suburbs.

Two cities that exemplify the move by Jews in the state from urban to suburban or city to town life are New Brunswick and Highland Park, which sit on opposite sides of the Raritan River and whose histories are inextricably linked. At one time, New Brunswick was home to the largest Sephardic Jewish community in the United States outside New York City. These Sephardic Jews were part of a larger, very active Jewish population in New Brunswick, which worshipped at temples such as Anshe Emeth, a congregation founded in 1859. In the 1950s the Sephardic congregation Etz Ahaim prepared to move to Highland Park because the city of New Brunswick was interested in redeveloping the land on which their congregation stood. In 1963 the new building was dedicated and Highland Park's suburban sensibility and single-family homes became magnets for Jews of all backgrounds

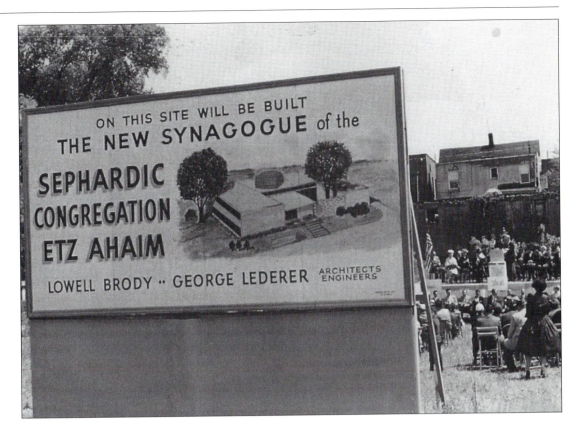

Breaking ground for the new Sephardic synagogue, Etz Ahaim, in Highland Park, circa 1960. *Congregation Etz Ahaim*

who formerly lived and worshipped in an increasingly decaying New Brunswick.

Today, the 1.8 square miles of Highland Park support a large Jewish community, with one Conservative and four Orthodox synagogues. Although New Brunswick has a thriving Hillel and Chabad House on the Rutgers University campus, the focus of Jewish community life definitively shifted across the river to Highland Park in the 1950s and 1960s. As such, this city and town, geographically so close, reflect the movement away from cities by Jews and their embrace of suburban life.

Like so many Americans, Jews were attracted to the same suburban "ideal" that shaped post–World War II American life: individual homes and workplaces surrounded by green space. Still, they often lost some of the community closeness that had been engendered by the physical proximity of urban density and the solidarity that is often a function of poverty and oppression.

THE SYNAGOGUE SALOON
OF GLOUCESTER CITY

The King Street Cafe, formerly Beth-El Congregation, Gloucester City.
Michael Aaron Rockland

Gloucester City is a small working-class city adjoining Camden. On King Street, down by the Delaware River, is an imposing structure called the King Street Cafe. However, above the cafe's awning is a marble stone inscribed with a Star of David and the words "Beth-El," Hebrew for "House of God," and just below it the words "Beth-El Congregation" in stained glass. Inside, a heavy-metal band is playing on the balcony where women once prayed, and above the bar is the huge mezuza that adorned the doorpost of the synagogue for fifty years (1930–80). Twelve-foot-high stained-glass memorial windows line the walls, letting in a gloriously colored light reminiscent of the Chagall windows in Jerusalem.

"Did you come to drink or pray?" the bartender jokes.

"Maybe a little of both."

"We named it wrong," the bartender continues. "This is a bar. We should have called it 'Bar Mitzvah.'"

Once King Street was lined with Jewish businesses, and Beth-El was the center of Jewish community life. Now the descendants of those congregants live largely on the other side of Camden in Cherry Hill. Some Jews endeavored to move the memorial windows to a temple there, but the town council of Gloucester City wished to keep them in place as part of the city's historic legacy.

However one may feel about converting a Jewish temple into a saloon, the owners of the King Street Cafe have conserved the key architectural features of Beth-El. To complicate the picture, 1 South King Street, erected in 1887, had a long life as a bank and then as the town post office before it became a synagogue, and after Beth-El moved it was twice an artist's studio. The building is a perfect example of the principle of adaptive reuse and stands in mute testimony to the fact that nothing withstands the changes wrought by time.

5

Jews on the Farm

THE FORMER JEWISH agricultural colonies are quiet now. Some have been abandoned, others sold off. The plain, wooden synagogues have mostly disappeared, though one is now a Baptist church. A shopping mall with a vast parking lot covers the site of one of the farming communities, condos most of another. A large portion of yet another has disappeared under the waters of a reservoir. At the site of one agricultural colony virtually nothing remains but a Jewish cemetery dedicated to "the first agricultural colonists who migrated from Russia to the woodlands of South Jersey."

Jewish farmers? For centuries Jews have tended to be seen, and even to see themselves, as anything but farmers—as if "Jewish farmer" were an oxymoron. This is because in virtually all the Pale of Settlement, to which Jews were restricted in Eastern Europe, they were specifically precluded by law and the church from owning land. As one New Jersey agricultural colony farmer put it, "My parents always remembered the black soil of Russia which they were not permitted to plow." Thus, despite fervent contrary desires, Jews perforce came to be identified with commerce and trade and to be thought of as people who would not work with their hands—a source of much vicious persecution. Only the modern State of Israel, which has made the desert bloom through

The Passaic County Live Poultry Dealers Association on January 3, 1926. Jews eventually constituted as much as 90 percent of the poultry and egg farmers in New Jersey.
Jewish Historical Society of North Jersey

ingenious agricultural methods, has reminded the world, and Jews as well, that farming from biblical days onward has been far from foreign to the Jewish nature.

But long before the State of Israel, Jewish farmers were prominent in New Jersey. Indeed, the poultry and egg industry was almost exclusively Jewish. By 1950, New Jersey's Jewish farmers had made Monmouth the number-one county in the nation in egg production, and New Jersey was widely known as "the egg basket of America." Jews were also prominent, and remain so, in New Jersey's dairy industry.

Despite the common stereotype of turn-of-the-century Jewish immigrants as Lower East Side denizens working in the needle trades, substantial numbers arrived in the United States with very different intentions. Some, in fact, from the first planned to live on and work the land. The novelist and editor of the *Jewish Daily Forward,* Abraham

Fanny Dubnik with chicks, Farmingdale Agricultural Colony, 1945. Because of her husband's heart condition, Fanny was the primary farmer in the family.
Gertrude Dubrovsky

Bessie and Max Goldman, immigrants from Russia and Poland, respectively, founders of New Jersey's large Farmland Dairy. They met in Paterson and decided they preferred a rural life to working in the mills, so they purchased a small farm. Beginning with thirty cows, they at first sold raw (unpasteurized) milk directly to consumers. Here they are on the family farm in Fairlawn, circa 1960.
Jewish Historical Society of North Jersey

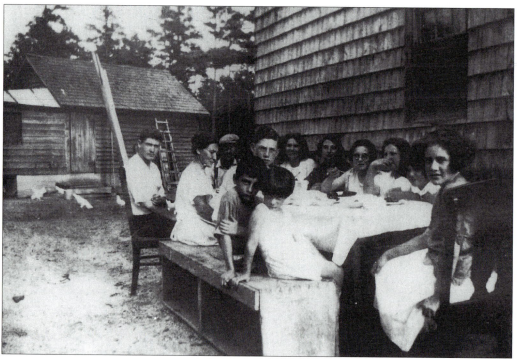

The Adolphe Blaine family enjoying a picnic at their farm near the Farmingdale Agricultural Colony in 1919. Adolphe, at the far end of the table, had suffered from tuberculosis and became a farmer partly to recover his health.
Gertrude Dubrovsky

Cahan, originally came to America planning to be a farmer. "The cities are full of many diseases that are unheard of on farms. Tuberculosis, for instance. . . . People in urban areas grow old and gray at forty, but most of the farmers are healthy and strong and live to be eighty and ninety," Cahan wrote.

New Jersey had the greatest number of Jewish farmers. While some forty Jewish agricultural settlements were founded around the nation— as far west as Colorado and Oregon and as far south as Louisiana— roughly thirty of them were in New Jersey. The New Jersey colonies were also the most substantial and long-lived, partly because they enjoyed the support of nearby Jewish institutions and philanthropists in New York and Philadelphia, but also because of the ready accessibility to the markets of those cities. One of the authors remembers Jewish farmers from New Jersey selling eggs door-to-door as a regular occurrence in the Bronx neighborhood of his childhood.

It was to reach markets that the first New Jersey agricultural colony, Alliance, was created in 1882 in close proximity to the Jersey Central rail line just outside Vineland. Many of its settlers had been, in Russia, members of the liberal Jewish organization Am-Olam, which advocated farming cooperatives, making Am-Olam a ready target of reactionary thinkers and the brutal pogroms they spawned after the assassination of Czar Alexander II in 1881. Alliance was soon followed by other, nearby Jewish colonies such as Carmel, Norma, Bortmanville, Hebron, Mizpah, and Rosenhayn, most in Salem and Cumberland Counties, so that by 1901 there were some 3,300 Jews living off the land in New Jersey. For these Jews, New Jersey's nickname, "The Garden State," came to have particular resonance.

The de Hirsch fund (a foundation created by European philanthropist Baron Maurice de Hirsch) and its subsidiary, the Jewish Agricultural Society, were instrumental in supporting Jewish agricultural colonies in Argentina, Canada, and the United States, but especially in New Jersey. As an employee of the fund stated, Jews "must be directed not to petty trades, not to the pushcarts or the pack on the shoulder, not to the tailor shop, but to the free, health-giving, ennobling, invigorating and plenteous farm life." And many Jewish farmers took to this work with

A Jewish farm family at Vineland dressed for Sabbath observance, circa 1890.
Gertrude Dubrovsky

enthusiasm, seeing farm life as the embodiment of emancipation. "Here I can be free, not the slave of others," one Jewish farmer wrote. "In America it is an honor to pay taxes." Said another, "I became a farmer because I didn't want to exploit anyone, but I didn't want to be exploited either. . . . In Russia . . . I was a revolutionary. . . . And what was the revolution? Not to be exploited."

Religious Jews especially found farm life attractive. As farmers, they required no special dispensation from an employer to abandon work on the Jewish Sabbath. What's more, feeding one's animals on the Sabbath is regarded as a permitted activity even among the most observant Jews.

A New Year's card, in Hebrew and German, sent by the farmer Samuel Stroger to his family back in Europe in 1905.
Gertrude Dubrovsky

Devoting oneself to agriculture and not congregating in cities was also thought to be a good way for Jews to combat anti-Semitism. The Jewish-American newspaper, *The Jewish Record*, felt in 1882 that settling on farms would be the most "effectual step to stamp out prejudice against the Jew." Rich German Jews, who had preceded Russian Jews to the United States by half a century, supported agricultural enterprise as

Samuel Stroger, who first farmed on Long Island, later joined the Farmingdale Agricultural Colony in New Jersey.
Gertrude Dubrovsky

a way to quickly "Americanize" their greenhorn Eastern European brethren and, though they were loath to admit this publicly, to simultaneously remove them from public scrutiny as a source of embarrassment. In addition, the farm could be an ideal place for immigrants with poor English skills. As a resident of one community put it, "Chickens understand German as well as they do English."

Prominent among the agricultural colonies created with support from the de Hirsch fund was Woodbine, in Cape May County, founded in 1891 with a purchase of 5,200 acres. In 1903, it became the first wholly Jewish incorporated political entity anywhere in the world since the destruction of the Second Temple in Jerusalem in 70 c.e. In 1894, the Baron de Hirsch School was founded at Woodbine, the first agricultural secondary school in America, with 270 acres of land, stables, and model dairy herds. At the dedication of a new classroom building in 1900, Rabbi Bernard Levinthal of Philadelphia stated, "Adam was placed in the Garden of Eden not to trade or peddle therein but to till it and to keep it."

The de Hirsch School was attended by as many as 100 potential Jewish farmers at a time, and a newspaper, *Der Yiddisher Farmer* (The Jewish Farmer), was published from 1907 to 1957 to support and instruct Jewish agriculturalists. A major street in the town of Woodbine today is de Hirsch Avenue. That it intersects with Jefferson Avenue seems appropriate, since Thomas Jefferson, in his celebration of the yeoman farmer, believed, not unlike de Hirsch, that living on and working one's own land is ennobling and fundamental to a free society.

But unlike American farmers who have typically lived in lonely isolation on widely scattered family farms, Jewish agricultural colonists often formed co-ops and lived in close proximity with each other, much like European farmers who to this day tend to live in towns and walk or tractor out to nearby fields. A Jewish agricultural colony was a community, much like a kibbutz or moshav in Israel. "If a farmer was sick, we all took turns taking care of his chickens," said one farmer.

The Jewish colonies built not only synagogues but schools and community centers where book clubs flourished, amateur theatricals were performed, and political discussion was vigorous. "Solving the problems

The co-op store at the Farmingdale Agricultural Colony. During the early 1950s, when Senator Joseph McCarthy was at the height of his power, the FBI investigated some Jewish agricultural settlements in New Jersey, seeing them as subversive seedbeds of radical thinking.
Gertrude Dubrovsky

of the lice [among their chickens] was easy," said a Farmingdale colony farmer, "but solving the Spanish Civil War! That was more complicated." And as another put it, "We existed by means of our farming, but we lived, we *lived*, because of our ideology."

Nevertheless, it may have been that very ideology and the cooperative spirit of many New Jersey farm communities that contributed to their eventual demise in a country supremely devoted to individualism

Hyman Grossman as an officer in the Russian army in 1914. By 1926 he was not only a farmer in New Jersey but the first president of the West Farms Jewish Community Center at Farmingdale.
Gertrude Dubrovsky

and capitalism. The quasi-socialism of the Jewish agricultural collectives dramatized the differences between Jewish farmers and their Christian neighbors. "We huddled together like chicks under a brooder stove," said Harry Sokol, an early settler at Farmingdale. Jewish farmers were often the objects of social ostracism or worse. Bricks were thrown through their front windows and crosses were burned on their front lawns by the Ku Klux Klan.

A sign for Hamburger's Colony at Farmingdale. Michael Hamburger first opened a vegetarian hotel and then expanded to include bungalows.
Gertrude Dubrovsky

A summer boarder from New York communing with a cow at Farmingdale.
Gertrude Dubrovsky

Sam Epstein worked on his chicken farm on Old Freehold Road in Dover Township in Ocean County for forty-four years. It was a seven-days-a-week job. "With criminals, they lock them up and throw away the key," Epstein often joked, "but with this farm, we locked ourselves in and threw away the key."
Photo by Rita Nannini, courtesy Leonard Epstein

Compounding the problems of Jewish farmers is that they usually arrived in America with less practical farming experience than other immigrants. Thus they were often mistaken about the quality of the land they chose to till and naive about the economics of farming and other practical matters. Sometimes the only reliable "cash crop" came from summer boarders—New York Jews seeking a bit of country life. Indeed, some of the farming communities became mini-resorts as much as farms, in the same manner Catskill Mountain hotels began as farms that took in boarders.

Ironically, Jews, stereotyped as urban dwellers, became farmers in the United States precisely when other Americans were leaving the family farm for better opportunities in the city. Nevertheless, perhaps because being farmers and landowners remained an attractive novelty to Jews, the Jewish Agricultural Society continued settling Jews on the land in New Jersey. Indeed, between 1946 and 1952, the JAS settled an additional 2,500–3,000 Holocaust survivors and displaced persons from Europe on small farms in New Jersey.

The mid-1950s were the peak years of prosperity for New Jersey Jewish farmers, but small family farms were soon becoming unmanageable for Americans all over the country. Often Jewish farms were lost because merchants, such as Ralston, supplied feed on credit, and when the price of chickens and eggs plummeted and farmers could not repay their debts, the feed merchants took over the farms.

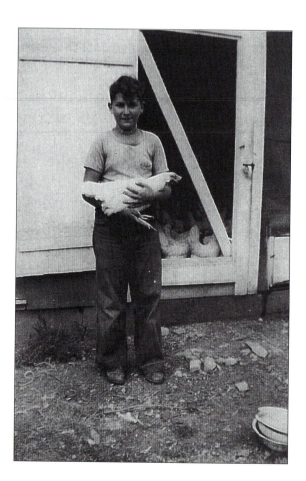

Gilbert Finkel as a child on the family chicken farm in Jackson Township. Finkel remembers being anything but enamoured of some of the farm work he did during the summers while going to college. "You took a shovel and, outside the coop, you took a big breath of air. Then you went in. The chicken shit was about two feet high. You got a shovel full and didn't breathe until you got outside and dumped it on the truck to be taken out to the field. The ammonia smell was awful. After a summer doing this, I knew there was no way I was going to take over the farm. I went back to college in the fall and enrolled in the food science courses."
Gilbert Finkel

Sam Epstein, the only member of his family to survive a Nazi mas-sacre in Drochichin, Poland—though with a bullet in his lung—tried working as a baker in New York when he immigrated in 1948 but then thought it might be healthier to be a farmer. He bought a chicken farm in 1950, one of thirty-eight along Old Freehold Road in Dover Township in Ocean County. With egg prices so low, his was the only chicken farm left by 1988. Condos stood where there had once been chicken coops. Epstein survived by selling his eggs directly to neighbors instead of going through ruinous middle men.

Jewish farms failed in New Jersey also because children shared nei-ther their parents' delight in farming nor their socialist idealism. Also, it can be said that Jewish farming in New Jersey was defeated by educa-tion. The children of immigrant farmers, for the most part, did not wish to be farmers. They went to college and then entered the profes-sions. But many of them maintained their connection to the agricul-tural world they were born into. Jacob Lipman grew up on a New Jersey chicken farm and studied at the de Hirsch School at Woodbine. After attending Rutgers University, he eventually became its first dean of the College of Agriculture. His pioneering studies in soil science helped change farming methods around the world.

Gilbert Finkel, of Morris Plains, grew up on a chicken farm in Jackson Township. His parents, immigrants from Lithuania, raised twenty-two thousand chickens on a twenty-acre farm where Gilbert worked as a boy. Later, when he went to college, he received three credits each summer for working on the farm. Upon graduating, how-ever, being a chicken farmer was the last thing he wanted to do. Never-theless, he did not stray far from his agricultural origins: today he is a food scientist.

George Segal never left the New Jersey chicken farm where he grew up in South Brunswick, where his immigrant parents settled when he was a boy. But it became clear to him early in life that he wished to be a sculptor, not a farmer. Soon he had converted the long, low chicken coops into a rambling series of studios, ensuring that his farming past was never entirely absent from his sculptural work. Indeed, it is key to understanding several of his major works.

George Segal's environmental sculpture *The Butcher Shop* features a life-cast of his mother chopping a chicken in a kosher butcher shop. It was created to honor his father, who was a butcher in the 1930s before becoming a chicken farmer.
Art Gallery of Ontario, Toronto

THE FARMER-SOLDIER

Bernard Bernkopf and his brother Heinrich (later Henry) grew up in Cologne, Germany. Their parents sent them to America in 1939, where they bought a farm near Berlin, New Jersey. When the United States entered World War II, both brothers enlisted and fought in the European theater. The much-decorated Bernard fought in the Battle of the Bulge and, after the Nazis surrendered, made his way to Cologne in 1945 to see if he could learn something of his parents' fate. As recounted in *Stars and Stripes* on March 9, 1945, by Andy Rooney (later of CBS's *60 Minutes*), after some initial hesitation, Bernard was "told in whispers" just where his parents "had been hidden by Gentiles while the Gestapo looked for them." His parents were as surprised to see Bernard as he was to find them miraculously alive. Continued Rooney in the newspaper, "There were tears in his father's eyes today as the two wandered through the ruins of Cologne arm in arm."

Bernard Bernkopf at his farm near Berlin, New Jersey, in 1943.
Tri-County Jewish Historical Society Collection
at the Camden County Historical Society

6

Roosevelt

IN ADDITION TO the agricultural settlements with their idealistic and communal qualities, Jews were prominent in various New Jersey utopian experiments as well. For example, the Modern School (1915–1955), in the Middlesex County town of Stelton, was an anarchist agricultural colony with a radically experimental school at its core, some 75 percent of whose 100 participant families were East European Jews. They rallied for Sacco and Vanzetti. They sang songs with lines such as, "One, two, three, pioneers are we / We're working for the working class against the bourgeoisie."

But among New Jersey's various exercises in utopianism, Roosevelt stands out, partly because it has, in one form or another, endured and partly because it has been made famous by its artists. Twelve hundred acres located a few miles southeast of Hightstown in western Monmouth County, Roosevelt was first known as Jersey Homesteads. Its plans were formulated in 1933, and families began to move there in 1936. The government built its spare, Bauhaus-style cinder block homes for those who could put up a $500 bond and for others on a purely rental basis.

Jersey Homesteads was one of ninety-nine subsistence farming projects around the country sponsored by the New Deal's National

Workers, circa 1936, building the standard, squarish, cement block house, inspired by Bauhaus ideas of simplicity, that is characteristic of Roosevelt even today.
Borough of Roosevelt Historical Collection, Special Collections, Rutgers University Libraries

Philip Goldstein, assistant cutter in the cooperative garment factory at Jersey Homesteads, circa 1936.
Borough of Roosevelt Historical Collection, Special Collections, Rutgers University Libraries

Jersey Homesteads women and children in the cultivated fields surrounding the settlement. This photograph was taken by the noted photographic artist Dorothea Lange for the WPA (Works Projects Administration) in 1936.
Borough of Roosevelt Historical Collection, Special Collections, Rutgers University Libraries

Roosevelt residents working in the fields, as photographed by Dorothea Lange for the WPA, circa 1936.
Borough of Roosevelt Historical Collection, Special Collections, Rutgers University Libraries

Recovery Administration, which sought means to relieve the misery of the Great Depression by providing employment and a measure of independence on the land to oppressed city people. But Jersey Homesteads was unique: it was expressly set aside for European immigrant Jews, it was a cooperative, and it combined agriculture with industry.

Most of its early settlers, when they could find employment, had worked in the needle trades in New York, so it was logical for them to transfer their skills to the small garment factory that was built at Jersey Homesteads to supplement agriculture, which provided only seasonal employment. The factory had its own retail store and advertised its wares widely. Ironically, the opposition to Jersey Homesteads included David Dubinsky, president of the International Ladies' Garment Workers Union, who regarded the rural New Jersey cooperative as undermining union solidarity. When Albert Einstein, who lived in nearby Princeton and was a supporter of Jersey Homesteads, remonstrated with Dubinsky, he reportedly said, "When it comes to physics, you're the professor. When it comes to labor, I'm the professor."

At one point Einstein also supported a plan to create a small college which, though never built, was typical of the idealistic projects that have always animated the spirit of the town. Nevertheless, despite high hopes for Jersey Homesteads among its residents and outside intellectuals, the garment factory was, year after year, unable to show a profit, and the cooperative poultry, dairy, and truck farms, despite government subsidies, eventually failed. The government auctioned off these properties, some of which were thereafter managed privately, and liquidated its involvement with the settlement's real estate by selling the homes outright to individual families. For years Jersey Homesteads was regarded by New Deal critics as a prime example of unrealistic, quasi-socialist excess.

The community showed where its own sympathies lay when, after World War II, it incorporated itself as a town and renamed itself Roosevelt to honor its benefactor. There is a huge bust of Franklin Roosevelt in the town park executed by the sculptor Jonathan Shahn, whose father, Ben Shahn, created an extraordinary mural that decorates a wall of the town school. These works of art are characteristic of what Roosevelt has

Ben Shahn (center) and friends in front of the Roosevelt Post Office, circa 1965.
Borough of Roosevelt Historical Collection, Special Collections, Rutgers University Libraries

been in recent decades: an idealistic community that has uncommonly championed liberal causes, and the closest thing to an artist's colony New Jersey has ever produced.

Ben Shahn, no doubt New Jersey's most distinguished graphic artist, settled in Roosevelt after he had painted his mural in 1936, drawn to what he considered the town's special spirit. Soon other prominent artists, attracted by Shahn's presence, made Roosevelt their home, including Jacob Landau, Gregorio Prestopino, and Stefan Martin. Opera singers and pianists also joined the community, as did Edward Roskam, a writer and photographer, who described Roosevelt as "a marvelous place for artists to work."

Roosevelt citizens demonstrating in Trenton against a proposed giant jetport, March 4, 1969.
Borough of Roosevelt Historical Collection, Special Collections, Rutgers University Libraries

Today Roosevelt's influence as an artist colony has waned some-what and its population is no longer overwhelmingly Jewish. Yet in its rustic charm, it sometimes still finds itself compared to a "shtetl," one of the small Jewish towns of pre–World War II Eastern Europe. Whether shtetl or not, it does seem to have an uncommonly strong community flavor, what a resident once described as "a little town where everybody is involved with everybody else." In 1983, Roosevelt was named to the National Register of Historic Places.

Jews at the Shore

"BAGEL BEACH" was Bradley Beach's nickname through the 1950s, suggesting the prominence of Jewish settlement there and the large numbers of Jews who flocked to its beaches in summer. Like New Jersey's cities and later its suburbs, the New Jersey shore has had its ethnic enclaves.

Bradley Beach is only one of the communities that is stamped with a Jewish presence along the 127-mile length of the New Jersey shore. There were Jews at the shore as far back as pre–Revolutionary War times, mostly peddlers and fishmongers. But it was wealthy German Jews who, in the mid- to late nineteenth century, came to Elberon and surrounding towns, including Long Branch, Deal, Sea Bright, and Allenhurst, and were the first to establish a sizable presence. With signs announcing "No Hebrews Taken" posted at many hotels, and with whole towns clearly, if discreetly, discriminatory, Jews needed such enclaves, as well as shore resorts such as the Atlantic Hotel in Long Branch that catered to Jews in the nineteenth century. Thus Jews initially lived and vacationed at the shore in largely segregated settlements.

Those settlements, with their dazzling array of elaborate Victorian summer residences, had something of the air of Jewish Newports. The famous banker Joseph Seligman, who helped the Union cause

Aaron Rassas, a fishmonger in Long Branch. Aaron's chant was "Fish fish, cheap as dirt, a little stink wouldn't hurt."
Alise Schlosser Ford

Pete Arnold and Marjorie Kohn Miller on Phillips Avenue in Deal, 1916.
Keith Miller

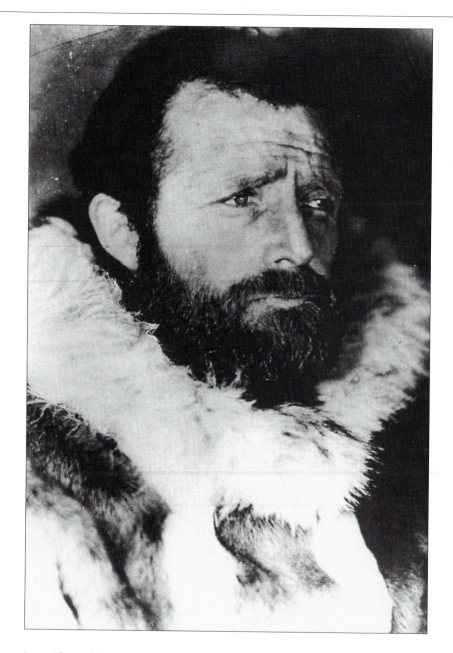

Isaac "Ike" Schlossbach, circa 1930s. Commander Schlossbach was a lifelong resident of Neptune, when he wasn't exploring with Admiral Richard Byrd in the Antarctic. A mountain in the Rockefeller Range in the Antarctic is named for him.
David Nussbaum

during the Civil War by selling government bonds abroad, bought a seaside "cottage" on Ocean Avenue in Long Branch in 1866. Publicly snubbed because of his religion at Saratoga's Grand Union Hotel, Seligman was glad to vacation at the somewhat more hospitable Jersey shore. Several of his brothers followed suit, including Jesse Seligman, who made Jews more socially acceptable through his friendships with Presidents Ulysses S. Grant and James A. Garfield. The latter's family stayed at Jesse's shore home while Garfield struggled unsuccessfully to recover from an assassin's wounds in 1881. Other wealthy New York Jews who were lured to the Jersey shore were the Guggenheims and Jacob Schiff.

Eastern European Jews followed the influx of German Jews to the shore, most living in modest circumstances. Kosher boarding houses arose to respond to their needs, and those who settled permanently at the shore opened restaurants, dry goods stores, and other establishments. Isaac "Ike" Schlossbach, who served in Richard E. Byrd's second scientific expedition to Antarctica, grew up in Neptune, where his family owned a dry goods store.

Max Gallner (center) and Nathan Fisher (back, right) with friends on the beach in Atlantic City, circa 1917. Max married Nathan's sister Ida in 1919. Atlantic City was a popular shore destination for Jews.
Paul Gallner

Joseph and Bessie Marcus and Abraham and Bessie Jelin, all from New Brunswick, on the Boardwalk in Atlantic City in the 1920s. Abraham Jelin was the state highway commissioner. Ruth Marcus Patt, the daughter of Joseph and Bessie Marcus, has written numerous books and pamphlets about the history of Jews in New Jersey and has served as president of the Jewish Historical Society of Central Jersey.
Jewish Historical Society of Central Jersey

Before synagogues were constructed, summer residents often attended services in houses rented by rabbis for the summer. Among the synagogues built was Temple Beth Miriam in Long Branch, named for Miriam Philips Meyer, wife of Sigmund Meyer, a local realtor. It was the first synagogue in the United States named for a woman.

Jews have long been as susceptible to the shore's attractions as others. Atlantic City, especially in the first half of the twentieth century, was a frequent destination of vacationing middle- and upper-middle-class Jews. It was also a favorite of the sporting class, some of whom, during Prohibition, had other things in mind than nature

Deenie Rassas Schlosser and her father, Joseph Rassas, on the Boardwalk in Atlantic City, circa 1934.
Alise Schlosser Ford

when they looked out to sea: they were searching the horizon for small boats unloading liquor from ocean-going vessels. Other towns had special Jewish characteristics, such as Belmar. From 1900 to the 1930s, Belmar was known for the Jewish intelligentsia who lived or vacationed there, including the Yiddish writer Sholom Aleichem.

The country's general affluence and declining anti-Semitism during and after World War II attracted more middle- and lower-middle-class Jews to vacation at the shore or to buy summer homes in areas outside the early Jewish enclaves. Philip Roth's family came to the shore, as did so many others, to escape the steaming summer heat of Newark. As he explains in *The Facts,* the small bungalows his family rented in Bradley Beach were "paradise for me, even though we lived three in a room, and four when my father drove down the old Cheesequake highway to see us on weekends or to stay for his two-week

Leslie Cohen and his father, Dr. Samuel Cohen, on the porch of their home on Pavilion Avenue in Long Branch, circa 1920s. Bessie Yawitz Cohen, Sam's wife and Leslie's mother, was a real estate agent in town and Dr. Cohen was a chiropractor. Like many year-round shore residents, the Cohens rented out rooms in their home during the summer.
Alise Schlosser Ford

vacation." Jewish vacationers like Roth occasionally experienced anti-Semitic incidents. But it is difficult to determine what portion of more recent Jewish segregation at the shore is self-segregation, not unlike the Irish in Spring Lake.

Adult communities such as The Villages in Howell Township, the majority of whose residents are Jewish, make up a significant segment of shore Jews today. Such communities are part of the suburbanization of shore towns, echoing this transformation elsewhere. The Jewish Federation of Greater Monmouth County, in its very title, suggests how much Jews have spread out in their settlement patterns along the Jersey shore.

Today, Sephardic Jews, notably those from Syria, are a significant presence at the shore. With the creation of the modern State of Israel in 1948, Jews who had for centuries lived in relative peace in Arab lands were menaced. Many Syrian Jews went to live in Israel, but others came

Mary Woda with son Mel, Lakewood, 1932. In the background is the Sons of Israel Orthodox synagogue that the Wodas attended. Lakewood, while not on the ocean, was a major vacation site of New Jersey Jews. Today it has a large Jewish community and what some consider the most distinguished yeshiva in North America, the Beth Medrash Govoha, founded in Lakewood in 1943.
Mel Woda

to America, especially to Deal, New Jersey. The Synagogue of Deal was founded in the 1940s and has greatly expanded over the decades as vacationers gradually turned into permanent residents. Syrian Jews have joined the Deal Casino swim club in great numbers and built yeshiva day and high schools as well as a mikveh and a home for the aged in Long Branch. Currently, there are several Orthodox Sephardic congregations in Deal, Long Branch, and the surrounding communities of Oakhurst and West End.

The beautiful homes of the Deal area harken back to the shore communities settled by German Jewish predecessors. And the towns of the shore still preserve a slower, small-town feeling even with all the area's development. New Jerseyans say they are going "down the shore," a phrase that suggests the different mentality of the place. Ultimately, however, Jews continue to have an affinity for the Jersey shore for the same reasons everyone else does—the ocean, the sand, and the air.

Celebration
and Education

FOR OVER FIVE THOUSAND YEARS, Jews have fol-
lowed a calendar marking seasonal celebrations as well as important
events in Jewish history. Such occasions foster solidarity and are a key
reason why Jews have survived as a people. The principal holidays—
Rosh Hashanah, Yom Kippur, Sukkot, Chanukah, Purim, Passover, and
Shavuot—foster tradition and remembrance and link New Jersey Jews
with the past and with their brethren around the world.

The Jewish calendar begins with Rosh Hashanah in early fall.
Emma Lazarus, part of whose poem "The New Colossus" appears on
the pedestal of the Statue of Liberty, wrote a Rosh Hashanah poem in
1882 that includes the lines, "When orchards burn their lamps of fiery
gold, / The grape glows like a jewel, and the corn / A sea of beauty and
abundance lies, / Then the new year is born." In the United States the
Jewish New Year coincides with the school year, fittingly enough for
Jews, who have always given particular emphasis to education, seeing
learning and religion as inseparable.

Rosh Hashanah celebrates God's creation of the world and the
power of God to judge us and, one hopes, inscribe us in the Book of
Life for the new year. Challah, apples, and honey are among the traditional foods of Rosh Hashanah, and symbolic of a sweet year. The

Purim party, Burlington, 1913. Pretending to be Queen Esther, Haman, and Mordechai has long been a favorite Purim activity of Jewish children in religious school pageants.
Tri-County Jewish Historical Society Collection at the Camden County Historical Society

emphasis on food, a necessity of life and one of its greatest pleasures, is for many Jews often their strongest association with each holiday. Thus, even with Yom Kippur (the Day of Atonement), the most solemn Jewish holiday, a day-long fast is broken with a feast. Five days after Yom Kippur, the joyous nine-day festival of Sukkot begins, in which Jews celebrate by partaking of their meals in huts decorated to celebrate the bounty of the harvest season. Chanukah has its potato latkes fried in oil, Purim its hamantashen, and Passover its unleavened bread, bitter herbs, hard-boiled eggs, and greens. Each of these foods has its religious symbolism, but each also underscores the Jewish sentiment that life is meant to be tasted and savored among family and its goodness and benefits shared.

Seder at Bergen County's Camp Merritt for World War I servicemen, circa 1917. The Passover seder is the oldest continuously celebrated religious ceremony known to humankind. It centers on the story of the Jews' deliverance from enslavement in Egypt, and employs foods rich with the symbolism of freedom, spring, and rebirth. Passover combines a religious story with food, family, and celebration; it is a joyful Jewish holiday and the favorite of many.
Jewish Historical Society of North Jersey

The Sabbath, celebrated from sundown Friday through nightfall Saturday, is another opportunity to celebrate the fruits of the earth. In a sense it is the most important Jewish holy day, linked to the idea that God created the earth in six days and rested on the seventh. "Rest" is meant to be spiritual as well as physical, a time to reflect on other than the temporal and everyday. The idea of *shabbat* reminds Jews of the rhythms of the earth and of purposes in our lives beyond fame and riches. The day of rest is a key religious idea that Jews gave the world and may also explain, in part, the traditional prominence of Jews in the

Bar mitzvah portrait of Jules Nelson, 1919, New Brunswick, Ahavas Achim Congregation (which later relocated to Highland Park). In recent years bar and bat mitzvahs have become elaborate, weddinglike affairs in the United States, more bar than mitzvah as the old joke goes. Books such as *Putting God on the Guest List,* by Jeffrey K. Salkin et al., have sought to counter the consumer aspects of American culture as reflected in bar mitzvahs. Bar and bat mitzvahs are one of the few, and often only, times that non-Jews attend temple services, and thus they serve as a means to educating non-Jews about Judaism.

Jewish Historical Society of Central Jersey

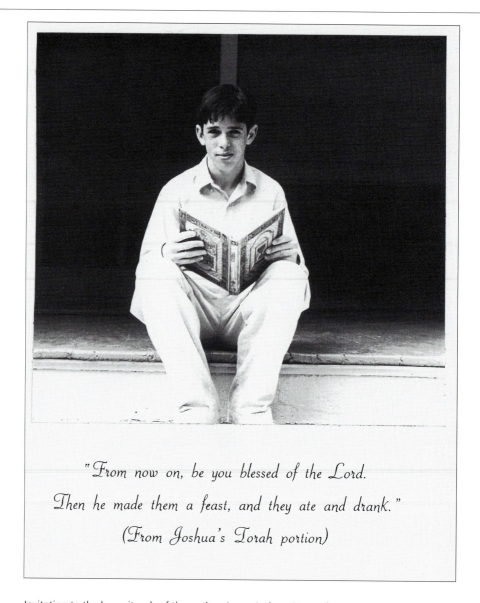

"From now on, be you blessed of the Lord.
Then he made them a feast, and they ate and drank."
(From Joshua's Torah portion)

Invitation to the bar mitzvah of the authors' son, Joshua, November 29, 1997, Temple B'nai Or, Morristown. Joshua's Torah portion was from Genesis and concerned Isaac's twin sons, Jacob and Essau, who God said represented "two nations."
Patricia M. Ard

American labor movement. The cup of wine used to sanctify the Sabbath is also suggestive of the Jews' appreciation for things of this earth. Wine and sexuality are both celebrated as not only holy but joyous and good in and of themselves. *L'chaim!* ("to life!") is for many Jews the most important Hebrew word in their personal lexicons, characteristic of Jewish attitudes toward nature and the very fact of existence. Thus,

Confirmation class, Temple Emanu-el, Paterson, May 1918. Before the modern feminist movement beginning in the late 1960s, Jewish girls rarely studied to become bat mitzvah but frequently had a confirmation.
Jewish Historical Society of North Jersey

Judaism eschews the puritanism that lingers in, if not actually charac-
terizes, so much of American culture.

Bar and bat mitzvahs, however, have been heavily influenced by
that culture. What were once simple, almost entirely religious affairs
have become so elaborate among upper-middle-class Jews in New Jersey
as to approximate weddings. American consumer culture mingles,
sometimes uncomfortably, with this ancient coming-of-age ceremony.
On the positive side, Jews in America have come to demand that their
daughters as well as their sons study and be honored as b'nai mitzvah; formerly, Jewish girls were only confirmed. Also, many contemporary Jewish prayer books have striven to be entirely gender neutral,
even as far as the deity is concerned, and the notion of a woman

Primary students learn to read Hebrew at the Jewish Educational Center, Elizabeth. Rabbi Pinchas M. Teitz (1908–95), the center's founder, helped to build a community of Jewish schools and temples in Elizabeth and was also actively engaged in international work in Israel and Russia.
Rivkah Blau

Newark High Street Y's day camp, circa 1950. Mixing Jewish stories with games has been a tradition in teaching Jewish history.
Jewish Historical Society of MetroWest

rabbi already shows signs of being so common as to be no longer a novelty.

An emphasis on study has given Jews the nickname the "People of the Book." As discussed earlier, Jews established schools almost immediately upon arrival in New Jersey. By the twentieth century, Jewish summer camps were combining play with Jewish education. Since New Jersey has a significant Orthodox population, Jewish day schools dot the state. In these schools as throughout Jewish history, study of the Torah, the first five books of the Bible, as well as the Talmud and the rest of the Hebrew Bible, is a prominent part of the curriculum. In *Proverbs,* Torah is called a "tree of life to those who hold fast to it," and the lively study of Torah in the Garden State is proof that Jews are, indeed, holding fast.

The pidyon ha-ben (redemption of the first born) ceremony of Charles Feldman, Elizabeth, 1944. As directed in Numbers 18:15–16, this ceremony is based on the tradition that the first-born male was supposed to serve at the holy altar of God's priests. Although later this function was transferred to the Levites and specifically the Kohanim, the sanctuary was still considered to have a claim on the first-born male. Therefore, on the thirtieth day after the child's birth, parents are commanded to "redeem" the child back from the Kohanim.
Charles Feldman

The Haggadah is another precious book for Jews, used to recount the Passover story each year. However, while the Torah never changes, American Jews occasionally produce special Haggadahs that reflect current stories of oppression and freedom involving both Jews and non-Jews. Thus, Passover has increasingly become a universal celebration, and each year one hears of more Christian churches that, partially in recognition of Passover's confluence with Easter and the fact that the Last Supper was a Passover seder, celebrate Passover as well.

Jewish tradition provides a framework for the key life events of birth, circumcision, b'nai mitzvah, engagement, marriage, and funeral.

Engagement photo of Fannie Hurvitz and Nathan Wolman, Princeton, circa 1916.
Patsy Braveman Endy

Sidney and Deenie Schlosser at their wedding, Newark, October 29, 1950. The Schlossers left the Conservative Morristown Jewish Center to found the Reform Temple B'nai Or. Their daughter Alise was the first child named in the new congregation, which initially held services in the Episcopal Church of the Redeemer on South Street.
Alise Schlosser Ford

Poster for Paterson Kunst group, advertising *All in a Lifetime*. Yiddish theater was a rich part of the cultural life of early twentieth-century New Jersey immigrants, especially in the major cities of the state.
Jewish Historical Society of North Jersey

Burning the mortgage is a joyous celebration for anyone. Here it is given ritual significance by Rabbi Reuben Kaufman of Temple Emanu-el, Paterson, burning the temple's mortgage, circa 1940.
Jewish Historical Society of North Jersey

Synagogues and temples are often settings for these occasions and many Jews join temples when they marry or have their first child, in order to have a Jewish community with which to celebrate and share their joys and sorrows. Temples are also where New Jersey Jews learn about Jewish community events such as fairs, concerts, and speakers on Jewish political or cultural themes of interest to Jews. Temples not only serve their own members but also, following Jewish custom, reach out into the larger community through working with local residents or church groups in soup kitchens and other socially conscious programs.

Judaism emphasizes spirituality and intellectuality, but does not neglect other aspects of a full life. Thus, Moses was a great thinker and

D'vorah Ohrbach and Abe Leibeskind in a Yiddish theater production, Paterson, circa 1930.
Jewish Historical Society of North Jersey

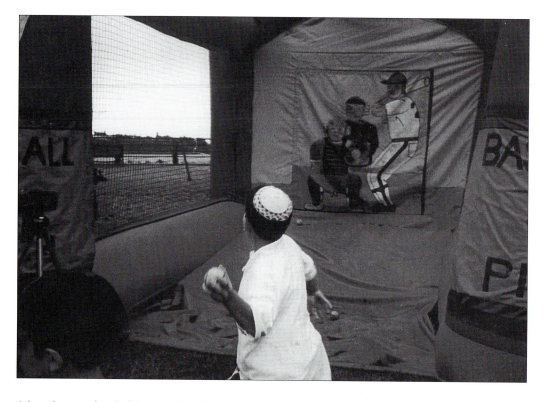

A boy throws a baseball in a stand at the annual Jewish Renaissance Fair, 1998, Liberty State Park, Jersey City. By the 1940s Jews were becoming as American as apple pie, producing such baseball greats as first baseman–slugger Hank Greenberg and, later, ace left-handed pitcher Sandy Koufax.
Rabbi Israel Teitelbaum, Rabbinical College of America

spiritual leader, but God named Joshua, the great warrior, as his successor. King David was a poet, but he also slew Goliath. Jews have continued this tradition of melding the temporal and the sacred in New Jersey. Jewish businessmen have existed side by side with Jewish scholars, and Jewish physicians with Jewish poets. As we write, the poet laureate of the United States, Robert Pinsky, and the poet laureate of New Jersey, Gerald Stern, are New Jersey–bred Jews. That's something to celebrate—not only as Jews but as New Jerseyans.

Anti-Semitism

The Snake in the Garden State

ALTHOUGH IT HAS NEVER approached the level Jews
experienced in Europe, anti-Semitism has been a presence throughout
New Jersey history. From the eighteenth through the middle of the
nineteenth century, when there were few Jews in the state, friction
between Jews and their fellow New Jerseyans was infrequent. However,
once Jews achieved a critical mass in the state, the centuries-old prejudice against them made itself felt. In the past, Jews have often been
reluctant to openly discuss anti-Semitism, fearing publicity might make
conditions worse. But the modern response to anti-Semitism has been
to publicize incidents in an effort to educate people about words and
acts that are considered unacceptable. While New Jersey has made great
strides, the state is among those with the highest level of incidents in
the nation. "There is a tendency [among Jews] to think it's not going on
in their backyards and it is. It's going on in everybody's backyard,"
observed Charles Goldstein, New Jersey's Anti-Defamation League
director in 2000.

In the late nineteenth and early twentieth centuries, the state's
"backyards" were rife with anti-Semitism. Hotels in the period often
had "No Hebrews" listed on their "welcome" signs. By the 1920s and
1930s, reflecting the international tide of bigotry against Jews, the

BAY VIEW HOUSE,

Centrally Located on the Water Front,

FIRST ESTABLISHED AND MOST POPULAR FAMILY HOUSE IN

Atlantic Highlands, New Jersey.

NO HEBREWS TAKEN.

An advertisement for the Bay View House in Atlantic Highlands, circa 1889, includes a proscription against Jewish guests— "No Hebrews Taken." The 1947 movie *Gentleman's Agreement,* based on the novel by Laura Z. Hobson, portrayed the prevalence of anti-Semitic exclusion in American public establishments such as hotels.

American Bund organization gained prominence. Fashioning itself into a local version of the Nazi party in Germany, the Bund had numerous chapters in such cities as Newark, Clifton, and Hackensack. Because of its nearness to Bund headquarters in Manhattan, a regional camp was established in Andover in Sussex County. Camp Nordland was a meeting place for American Nazis, led in the 1930s by Fritz Kuhn, assisted by the Bund's New Jersey leader, August Klapprott. Kuhn stated that Camp Nordland was a place where German American adherents of Nazism would be "strengthened and confirmed in National Socialism so that they will be conscious of the role which has been assigned to them as the future carriers of German racial ideals to America." Most New Jerseyans were horrified by the Bund's activities and, in an attempt to impede their activities, the New Jersey legislature passed a 1939 law prohibiting "violence or hostility" against anyone based on race or religion.

Other institutions were more subtle in their anti-Semitism. For example, Princeton University, like many Ivy League schools, instituted quotas for Jewish students that were not rescinded until well after World War II. In Ernest Hemingway's 1926 novel *The Sun Also Rises,* a central character, Robert Cohn, is a Jew who had attended Princeton.

A Bund rally of over one thousand marching American Nazis in Andover on July 18, 1937. Andover, a small town in Sussex County, was the site of Camp Nordland, a one-hundred-acre meeting place for American Nazis in the period before the United States' entry into World War II. A number of New Jersey citizens were leaders in the Bund organization, which was based in New York but had chapters all over the country. Most German Americans viewed these American Nazis with disgust and dissociated themselves from the group.
Associated Press

Cohn became a boxing champion at Princeton, even though he disliked the sport. Boxing allowed Cohn to "counteract the feeling of inferiority and shyness he had felt on being treated as a Jew at Princeton. . . . No one had ever made him feel . . . any different from anybody else, until he went to Princeton," Hemingway wrote.

When anti-Semitism forced Albert Einstein to flee Germany, he became director of the School of Mathematics of the Institute for Advanced Study in Princeton, which had been created by New Jersey Jewish philanthropists Louis Bamberger and his sister Caroline Bamberger

Fuld. "We have no other means of self-defense than our solidarity," Einstein warned his fellow Jews. Einstein's international fame, and his unflagging efforts before and during World War II to assist Jewish refugees, helped lessen anti-Semitism in New Jersey and the nation. By 1988 Princeton University had selected its first Jewish president, Harold T. Shapiro.

Jewish residents moving from the state's cities to the suburbs in the first half of the twentieth century regularly encountered anti-Semitic redlining by realtors; Jewish children were called "Christ Killers" and

Albert Einstein talking with members of the Princeton University Student Hebrew Association, founded in 1947. Einstein came to New Jersey to escape the vicious anti-Semitism of his native Germany and became a champion of Jewish and other human rights in New Jersey.
Princeton University Library

A Jewish man in 1994 makes his way among tombstones desecrated with Nazi swastikas and graffiti in a Jewish cemetery in the Passaic Junction section of Saddlebrook. One of the tombstones has been marked with the words "Hitler Was Right." Desecration of Jewish tombstones and temples is one of the primary means by which anti-Semitic sentiments are expressed in contemporary New Jersey.
Jewish Historical Society of North Jersey

experienced other slurs in school playgrounds. Today, incidents of anti-Semitism are tracked by the local Anti-Defamation League office. In December 1970 a campaign in Princeton attempted to force the public schools to cease their focus on Christmas to the exclusion of non-Christian holidays. Someone threw a brick through the front window of the home of the Jewish leader of the campaign; that same night there was a cross burning in a Princeton park. Another incident in 1999 involved a Barnegat Township school board member who resigned after referring to a former board member with an anti-Semitic slur.

Desecration of Jewish gravestones and anti-Semitic graffiti on temple walls still are seen too often in the state. And there are country clubs that exclude Jews, at best admitting one or two tokens to deflect charges of bias. But in the post-Holocaust world, anti-Semitism is openly combated and those who further it are publicly confronted. And

A hooded demonstrator protesting against the rally on July 4, 2000, in Morristown of Richard Barrett and his Nationalist Movement, which is linked to the Ku Klux Klan, white supremacists, and Holocaust deniers. There was also a huge interfaith protest against Barrett and his followers the evening before at which Cantor Bruce Benson of Temple B'nai Or led the Morristown community in joyous songs of solidarity.

Michael Aaron Rockland

one can point to many successes: the public schools no longer favor Christianity to the detriment of other religions, and the election of Frank Lautenberg, a Jew, to three terms in the United States Senate is surely a sign that Jews are more accepted as full citizens by the great majority of New Jerseyans. New Jersey is now the most ethnically diverse state in the nation, and increasingly Jews feel comfortable as participants in that mix.

The Holocaust
and Its Aftermath
in New Jersey

THE HOLOCAUST has had constant reverberations in America, in part due to the refugees and survivors who escaped the Nazis and later contributed to the cultural, political, economic, and everyday life of this country. We have selected a few who came to New Jersey and whose stories are especially moving. What makes these stories particularly poignant is the certain knowledge that these people would never have had the opportunity to contribute to American and New Jersey life and to continue their family lines but for a few, all too unusual, accidents of fate.

Abraham Zuckerman

The reader may have caught a glimpse of Hillside's Abraham Zuckerman at the end of the 1993 Steven Spielberg film *Schindler's List*, placing a stone on Oskar Schindler's grave in Jerusalem. Zuckerman was one of the *Schindlerjuden,* Jews who were saved from the death camps through the efforts of Schindler, who employed some twelve hundred Jews in real and bogus jobs.

Zuckerman, born in Krakow, Poland, lost his entire family in those death camps. From age fourteen until he was twenty Zuckerman was in no fewer than six camps, surviving by faking and later acquiring skills as

Abraham Zuckerman, born 1924, as a boy in Krakow, Poland, age ten. Note Hasidic garb and hairstyle. Zuckerman remains a very observant Jew today.
Abraham Zuckerman

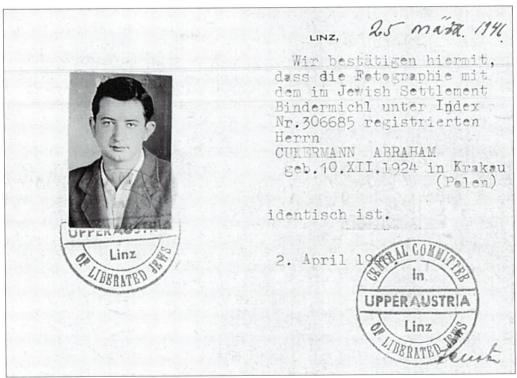

LINZ,   25 märz. 1946

Wir bestätigen hiermit,
dass die Fotographie mit
dem im Jewish Settlement
Bindermichl unter Index
Nr.306685 registrierten
Herrn
CUKERMANN ABRAHAM
    geb.10.XII.1924 in Krakau
                    (Polen)

identisch ist.

2. April 19...

Abraham Zuckerman's identity card in 1946, stamped by the Central Committee of Liberated Jews of Upper Austria, with headquarters in Linz. Zuckerman was assigned to the Bindermichl displaced persons camp.
Abraham Zuckerman

The marriage of Abraham and Millie Zuckerman in the Bindermichel displaced persons camp in Austria in 1947.
Abraham Zuckerman

an electrician. Contrary to the impression given by Spielberg's movie, not all the Jews on Schindler's list ended the war in his care. In Zuckerman's case, his time with Schindler, after internment at the fourth camp, fortified him both physically and spiritually to withstand the horrors of two more camps, Mauthausen and one of its satellites. After the war, Zuckerman testified at a trial of Nazi camp guards and kapos held at Dachau.

During the war, Zuckerman's future wife, Millie, and her family were hidden by brave Polish Christians in their attic, where they could vanish under the floorboards if the need arose, as it did on one notable occasion when Nazis searched the attic. The family lived an Anne Frank–like existence, though fortunately without discovery, until the end of the war. Millie and Abraham met and were married in the Bindermichel displaced persons camp in Austria in 1947.

By 1949, Abraham had lived in displaced persons camps for four years. As he explains in his book, *Memories of a Teenager Saved by*

Schindler, "I was a young person. I spent my teen years—six years—under guard and torture. . . . I had been liberated—but to do what? To go where?"

Fortunately, Millie had family in America. When Abraham and Millie arrived in the United States, they shared an apartment in Newark with Millie's parents. A year later, Abraham went into business with his childhood friend Murray Pantirer, also a *Schindlerjude.* It is both ironic and moving that these men, who had witnessed so much evil and destruction, became builders. Their company, LPZ (the initials of their surnames and that of yet another Holocaust survivor), is located in Union, New Jersey.

Millie Zuckerman, third from right, upon arrival in America in 1949, posing with family members. She is holding the Zuckermans' first child, Ann, who was born in the Bindermichel displaced persons camp in Austria in 1949.
Abraham Zuckerman

Oskar Schindler beneath a street sign bearing his name in one of LPZ's New Jersey developments, circa 1970. LPZ's offices in Union are located in Schindler Plaza. There is a bust of Schindler in the lobby and brochures for visitors in which Schindler is described as "The Humanitarian Who Cheated Hitler." Schindler, who was technically a member of the Nazi Party, is quoted in the brochure thus: "I hated the brutality, the sadism and insanity of Nazism. I just couldn't stand by and see people destroyed. I did what I could, what I had to do, what my conscience told me I must do. That's all there is to it. Really. Nothing more."
Abraham Zuckerman

In each of LPZ's developments there is a street named for Oskar Schindler, which makes these streets something like shrines. Developments with streets named for Schindler are found in South Plainfield, New Providence, Union, Berkeley Heights, Brick Township, Bridgewater Township, East Brunswick, Old Bridge, Randolph, Rockaway, Roxbury, and Washington Township. Oskar Schindler visited some of these sites when, on a trip to America, he stayed with the Zuckermans at their home. The Zuckermans also were reunited with Schindler in Jerusalem on one occasion and visited the Western Wall together.

Oskar Schindler and Millie and Abraham Zuckerman strolling in front of the Western Wall in Jerusalem. Schindler, honored at Jerusalem's Yad Vashem Holocaust Memorial as a "Righteous Gentile," died in 1974 and is buried in Jerusalem. The final scene of *Schindler's List* takes place there, with living survivors as well as the actors who played them in the movie filing past and, following Jewish custom, placing a stone on Schindler's grave.
Abraham Zuckerman

Jacob and Leah Weiss

Jacob Wajs (later Weiss) was born in Pziecsno, Poland; his wife, Leah (originally called Janka), was born in Krakow. Both somehow survived both the Auschwitz and Bergen-Belsen concentration camps but never met in either place. All their lives they carried on their arms the tattooed numerals they received in the camps.

Jacob and Leah met after the war while waiting in line for medical treatment in Bergen-Belsen, which had ironically been converted into a displaced persons camp—as was the case with several of the other death camps. They were married on December 18, 1947, in Bergen-Belsen;

Jacob and Leah Weiss in 1947, possibly on the day of their marriage in the Bergen-Belsen displaced persons camp, formerly a concentration camp.
Gloria Weiss Allen

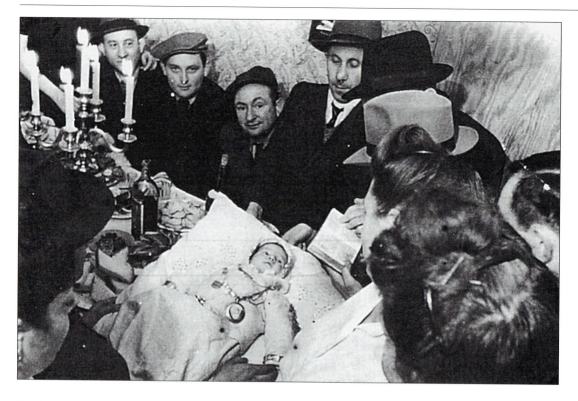

The *brit mila* (circumcision) of Mark Weiss in 1949 in the Bergen-Belsen displaced persons camp.
Gloria Weiss Allen

their first child, Mark, was born there in 1949, with his brit mila (circumcision) also celebrated in the displaced persons camp.

Like Abraham and Millie Zuckerman, the Weisses continued living in a displaced persons camp for several years after the war, since they had lost their families and did not know where to go. They tried briefly to live in Israel, but Leah found the heat oppressive.

Finally, in 1951, sponsored by the Morristown Jewish Center, they came to the United States and lived in the Jacob Ford Village garden apartments in Morristown. Jacob secured work as a tailor in various shops, including Epstein's Department Store, still located on the town Green. Eventually, the Weisses saved enough money to buy a home.

Jacob and Leah's second child, Gloria, was born in Morristown in 1953. Jacob and Leah would never speak with their children about their experiences in the camps. Nevertheless, as a child, Gloria memorized her mother's tattoo number and would chant it regularly like a kind of mantra.

The Weiss family in Morristown, circa 1959.
Gloria Weiss Allen

Gloria Weiss Allen lives to this day in the home her parents bought years ago. "I couldn't bear to sell it," she says. She and her family attend the same temple, the Morristown Jewish Center, that sponsored her parents when they came to America some fifty years ago.

Ruth B. Mandel

Ruth B. Mandel (née Blumenstock) was born in Vienna in August 1938, less than three months before *Kristallnacht* (Night of Broken Glass, November 9–10, 1938). After that night, Jews living under the Reich could have had little doubt that there was no future for them there. This was underscored when Ruth's father, Michael, was arrested and placed in the Dachau concentration camp, as were thousands of other Jewish men.

Ruth's mother, Lea, worked frantically to secure her husband's release, which, through bribery and other means, was still possible in those days when official Nazi policy advocated the forced emigration of Jews rather than their slaughter. When Michael Blumenstock was finally released, his wife urged him to flee to China, but he refused to

Ruth Blumenstock as an infant with her mother, Lea, and her grandmother, Jeneta Schmelzer, late 1938 or early 1939.
Ruth B. Mandel

Ruth Blumenstock held in her father's arms aboard the Hamburg-American line's ship *St. Louis*. Michael Blumenstock had recently been released from Dachau and shows obvious signs of his ordeal there.
Ruth B. Mandel

This photograph/card was sent by Ruth Blumenstock and her parents from England when she was five years old to her maternal grandparents, who had escaped Europe and were living in the United States.
Ruth B. Mandel

go without his family. He attempted to make his way to Belgium but was turned back at the border and returned to Austria. Finally, the family decided to book passage on the ill-fated *St. Louis* of the Hamburg-America Line. In May 1939 they set sail for Havana, Cuba, where they had been led to believe they would receive sanctuary.

Their hopes and those of the 917 mostly Jewish passengers aboard the *St. Louis* were dashed when the Cuban government refused entry on a technicality. The *St. Louis* then attempted entry into the United States, remaining off the coast of Miami for several days until it was clear the U.S. government was turning a deaf ear to their pleas. The reason? The

Ruth Mandel (right) in her role as director of the Center for the American Woman and Politics, with Hillary Rodham Clinton at Rutgers University, during Bill Clinton's first campaign for president in 1992.
Ruth B. Mandel

Four generations: Ruth Mandel, her mother, Lea, her daughter, Maud, and Maud's baby, Lev Michael Simon, in New Jersey in July 2000.
Ruth B. Mandel

passengers did not come under the strict per-country immigrant quotas that had been in effect since the 1920s. To its enduring shame, the United States refused to make exceptions for people who, if not admitted, were likely to face death—not to mention that these quotas were meaningless given that the Jews had been made, in effect, noncitizens of their respective countries under Nazi law.

The *St. Louis* sailed back to Europe where, in June, the passengers were accepted in almost equal numbers into France, the Netherlands, Belgium, and Great Britain. Luckily, the Blumenstocks were among those welcomed into Britain. Refugees would find their presence in the other three countries no refuge at all when the Nazis invaded Western Europe in 1940, and many of them ended up deported to the death camps. It is generally estimated that only about half of the 917 passengers aboard the *St. Louis* survived the Holocaust. Their story is told in detail in the book *Voyage of the Damned*.

In England, Ruth Blumenstock and her family first lived in Spalding, where her father worked as a gardener before entering the British Army. After the war, the Blumenstocks emigrated to the United States in 1947. Ruth has spent much of her adult life in New Jersey as a professor at Rutgers University. She was the founding director of the Center for the American Woman and Politics and is presently director of the Eagleton Institute of Politics at Rutgers, which includes the center. She was appointed by President Bill Clinton as vice chairperson of the Council of the United States Holocaust Memorial Museum in Washington. Illustrative of the continuity of generations, her daughter, Maud Strum Mandel, is a professor with a specialty in modern Jewish history.

Hans Fisher

Hans Fisher, who was born in Breslau, Germany (now Wroclaw, Poland), in 1928, was also aboard the *St. Louis,* but his experience varies in notable details from that of Ruth Mandel. He recalls suffering the taunts and beatings of Hitler Youth members and looking out his apartment window in 1938 as Adolf Hitler rode by in a motorcade. Still, his paternal grandfather counseled patience, incapable of believing it necessary to leave his homeland when four of his sons had died fighting for Germany during World War I.

The morning after Kristallnacht, Fisher's father was arrested and incarcerated in the Buchenwald concentration camp. He was released when he obtained a Cuban visa and sailed there, with the expectation that his family would follow soon on another ship. But by the time the *St. Louis* arrived with Hans and his mother and sister, Cuba was no longer admitting refugees. Hans remembers the pain of being anchored just off Havana and his father calling to him to no avail from a small boat below.

When the *St. Louis* returned to Europe, the Fishers were among those admitted to France, and Hans was temporarily placed in a children's camp on the outskirts of Paris. But with the advent of World War II on September 1, 1939, the Germans began bombing France and, it was clear, would soon invade. Endeavoring again to leave Europe, the Fishers

Hans Fisher, his sister Ruth, and his mother, Johanna, in Breslau circa 1933.
Hans Fisher

Hans Fisher (standing, far right) with other boys aboard the *St. Louis*.
Hans Fisher

obtained Cuban visas a second time and boarded an antiquated ship, most of whose passengers were Spanish republicans who had escaped into France from Franco's Spain. In New York the Fishers were temporarily taken to Ellis Island. A few days later they boarded another ship for Cuba, where this time they gained admission and were united with Hans's father. A year afterward they came to the United States, where Hans's bar mitzvah was soon celebrated.

Hans's father was unable to obtain work in New York, so the family, after attending agricultural training for Jewish refugees in Bound Brook, moved to South Jersey and bought a small chicken farm in Vineland. Hans does not remember the years of farming with any affection. "My father was old," he says, "and he didn't know a chicken from a cow; he had two left hands. My father took care of the feed and the books, but I handled much of the work with the chickens. I became a good plumber; still am. My mother and I got jobs off the farm, but the money we earned went down the black hole of the farm. The farm never really was profitable. And when my father died it was $18,000 in debt."

Hans Fisher in the United States in his bar mitzvah suit.
Hans Fisher

Hans Fisher addressing a fiftieth anniversary reunion in 1989 of passengers on the *St. Louis* who survived the Holocaust.
Hans Fisher

Nevertheless, Hans, who came to America without one word of English, went on to become valedictorian of his high school class and, later, to be a professor of nutritional sciences at Rutgers University. In a sense he never left the farm because one of his specialties, for which he is world renowned, is animal feeds.

Hans Fisher has remained active in Jewish affairs, honoring the memory of Holocaust victims, survivors, and escapees any way he can.

Vera Nussenbaum

Vera Nussenbaum (née Ribetski) began life placidly enough in Leipzig, Germany, in 1925, though her father died when she was two and a half of natural causes. She went to school like any German girl. But soon the Nuremberg Laws were imposed and she was forced into a school restricted to Jews.

Vera Nussenbaum's first grade class in Leipzig with children of all backgrounds. Vera is seated at the far left in the first row.
Vera Nussenbaum

Vera Nussenbaum and her Jewish classmates in the restricted school after the Nuremberg racial laws were imposed. Vera is in the second row, far left.
Vera Nussenbaum

Vera Nussenbaum was saved from the Holocaust by means very different from those New Jerseyans discussed thus far: the Kindertransport Program. She was one of ten thousand mostly Jewish children who left Germany for Great Britain after Kristallnacht and before the beginning of World War II less than a year later, when the borders were sealed. That these children were saved, considering that 1.5 million of the 6 million Jews murdered in the Holocaust were children, is one of the few bright spots in an otherwise dark tapestry.

Vera's travel was organized from Leipzig through Berlin to Rotterdam, Holland, by train. She remembers to this day the German soldiers "laughing at us and taunting us as we passed through Berlin and then, in contrast, crossing the Dutch border where people were waiting for us with milk and cookies."

Vera Nussenbaum and her mother, Yetta Ribetski, shortly before Vera departed Leipzig in 1938 as part of the Kindertransport Program. Vera would never see her mother again.
Vera Nussenbaum

Vera Nussenbaum (waving) arriving in England. This picture was to become one of the most famous documents of the Kindertransport Program and has been reproduced in many books, films, and exhibits.
Vera Nussenbaum

Vera was placed aboard the very first Kindertransport ship, which arrived in Harwich, on England's east coast, on December 2, 1938. "I was frightened and lonely," she remembers, "but my mother told me she would join me in England in a few weeks, and I always believed my mother. I never saw her again." Vera now had no mother or father, and she had no siblings. She was alone in the world at age twelve. When asked whether she considers herself a survivor or an escapee, Vera said, "Some tell me I'm an escapee, but if you're in a burning house and your mother throws you out the window, you're a survivor."

At first Vera remained in Dovercourt, formerly an adult camp in Dover, England. But soon she was chosen as a foster child by an English family ("lovely people," Vera says), with whom she was to remain for more than eight years in Norwich. One day, a first cousin who was in the U.S. army came to her door and said he would bring her to America. "It was terrible for my adoptive mother," Vera says, "but for me it was exciting, an adventure. Also, I wanted to be where I could live a Jewish life and there were almost no Jews in Norwich."

In March 1947, Vera came to the United States and took up residence with her cousin's family. That summer she found a job in Camp Leni Lenape, named for New Jersey's most prominent Native American nation, and there met her future husband, Seymour Nussenbaum, a World War II veteran. In 1960, the Nussenbaums bought a home in Old Bridge, New Jersey, on the G.I. Bill and have lived there ever since.

In 1989, Vera attended the fiftieth reunion of living Kindertransport participants in England. While staring at the now-famous photo of her arrival in England (Vera had become a kind of poster child for the Kindertransport Program), she became aware of two women standing

Vera Nussenbaum's identification card after entering the United States as a resident alien in 1947. Note that her name has been shortened to Ribet from Ribetski. Her cousin's family in the United States had taken that name, so it seemed appropriate for her to take it as well.
Vera Nussenbaum

Vera Nussenbaum (center) and the two women who were her companions at the rail of the Kindertransport ship. This photograph was taken in 1989 at a fifty-year reunion in England. The three women are in the same order as in the shipboard picture.
Vera Nussenbaum

on either side of her who were also staring at the photograph. The three women began to talk and quickly realized that they were the people in the photograph. They had had no contact in half a century.

Vera's granddaughter, Mariel Meth, at the identical age as Vera when she left Germany on the Kindertransport, wrote a poem called "My Grandma." One verse reads:

> I can't imagine what it was like to live through the Holocaust when
>   you were a teen,
> My grandma knows, for she lost her family during that horrible scene.
> She knows what it feels like to lose your life before it really had a
>   chance to grow.
> So she made a promise to rebuild her life, in every way she could
>   know.

Marlene Stevens

Marlene Stevens (née Malka Lancman) represents yet another way some Jews escaped the Holocaust to eventually become New Jerseyans. She was born in Sanok, in eastern Poland, in 1939, the same year Russia

The remaining members of the Lancman family in a Siberian labor camp. Marlene is in the front row on the left, holding a doll.
Marlene Stevens

Foehrenwald Displaced Persons Camp, Germany, 1946. This photograph was taken on the occasion of a visit of the Catholic War Services, which brought a truckload of supplies. The man holding the Jewish flag is Julius Minzer, assistant director of the camp. Marlene Lancman is holding a Ping Pong paddle and is the third child from the right in the front row.
Museum of Jewish Heritage, gift of Evelyn Cohen

Marlene Lancman (right), her mother, and a younger sister just after the family had emigrated to the United States.
Marlene Stevens

Rob Stevens, son of Marlene and David Stevens, on a pilgrimage to the Madjanek concentration camp shortly after his father's death in 1995.
Rob Stevens

and Germany invaded that country from both sides. Luckily, as it turned out, the family had no passports. Those without passports were deported by the Russians to Siberia when the Germans swept east in 1941, while those with passports remained in Poland where they became victims of the Nazis.

On the way to Siberia, two of the Lancman children were lost and another died. Marlene's earliest memory is of her father making a box to bury her baby sister. The family spent the war years in a labor camp, only 300 of whose 1,200 inmates survived.

When the war ended, the Lancman family got out of Russia using forged papers and made their way west, ending up in the Foehrenwald displaced persons camp in Germany in 1945. They remained in the camp until 1948, when they emigrated to the United States, eventually settling in New Jersey. Marlene married David Stevens and settled in Short Hills. David, as a child, had escaped the Lodz ghetto in Poland but was later captured and sent to the Madjanek concentration camp, where, although repeatedly beaten, he was one of the rare survivors. David and Marlene's son Rob graduated in 2000 from Rutgers University, where he was a student of one of the authors of this book.

The Continuity of
New Jersey Jewish Life

JEWS FIND THEMSELVES on the horns of a particularly American dilemma: how to achieve full acceptance from their fellow citizens while not being absorbed through assimilation; how to maintain their integrity as a people while insisting that they are, at the same time, fully American. This dilemma faces all ethnic groups, but for Jews, who constitute both a religion and a people, the struggle is perhaps more intense. America asks a lot of Jews; Jews ask a lot of America.

The news media are full of alternately encouraging and discouraging stories about the future of the Jews in the United States and in New Jersey. One day we learn that anti-Semitism continues to decline. The next day we learn that intermarriage continues to skyrocket. Of course, there is an intimate correlation between such stories. Intermarriage, with regard to Jews or any other people, always increases as hatred declines. It suggests an unhappy question: is Jewish solidarity, and even survival, dependent on a certain amount of persecution? Is it possible that what the Nazis could not annihilate through murder is, in America, disappearing through love?

We do not think so. The Jewish community is not disappearing, just changing. In our research for this book we encountered great vitality in New Jersey Jewish life, both in the respect the Jewish community is accorded and in its own pride. And if some Jews have left the fold, there has been an increasing tendency for non-Jews to embrace Judaism. At our family's Reform temple the expression, "Funny, she/he doesn't look Jewish" would be too much of a commonplace to bear mentioning.

At the same time, there has been an immense growth in the ranks of Orthodox Jews and of Hasidim, who have no fewer than twenty-two Lubavitch communities in New Jersey, including a major center of activity at the Rabbinical College of America in Morristown. There are clear signs in the Jewish community of a craving for and a return to tradition. The nomination of an Orthodox Jew, Senator Joseph Lieberman, as the Democratic candidate for vice president in 2000 was especially significant because many people, Jews and non-Jews alike, had probably assumed that the first Jew nominated for such high office would be a liberal or secular Jew, someone who happened to be Jewish rather than one who identified so strongly and publicly with Jewish tradition. On the New Jersey college campuses where we teach, one frequently encounters new Jewish immigrants from the former Soviet Union and sees more male students each year wearing yarmulkes. There is a sense that in New Jersey today, being Jewish or "different" in any way is normal and does not require apology or even explanation.

Included here is a brief portfolio of photographs demonstrating the vitality and continuity of New Jersey Jewish life. It gives us pleasure to share them, and their associated stories, with the reader.

The inclusion of women in all aspects of Jewish worship—especially among Reform, Conservative, and Reconstructionist Jews—is certainly a major change in the character of American and New Jersey Jewish life. Increasingly, the deity is not gendered in Jewish prayer books and women pursue careers as rabbis. In this picture, women of the Jewish Center of Princeton parade around the temple on September 21, 1997, to celebrate the consecration of three new Torah scrolls.

The Jewish Center of Princeton

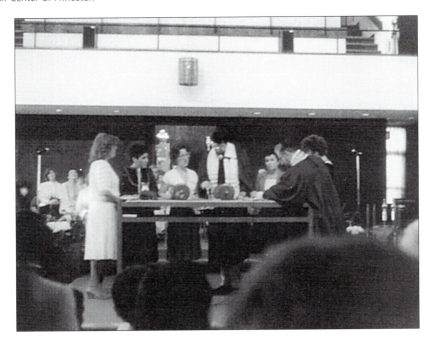

Other ways in which women participate more in Jewish worship is through their inclusion in a minyan, wearing a prayer shawl (tallit) and yarmulke, and, of course, through bat mitzvahs, which Jewish girls now celebrate almost as often as Jewish boys celebrate their bar mitzvahs. But many adult women grew up when this was not the case. At Temple B'nai Or in Morristown, special b'nai mitzvah were celebrated on June 13, 1981, for thirty-six adults, most of them women, who had been studying Hebrew for a year with the temple's rabbis. In the photograph, several of the celebrants are shown reading passages from the Torah.

Donna Parris

Three generations of Jewish women, Vivienne Cohen, of Springfield, her mother, Mildred Raphael, and her daughter, Jody Cohen, at Jody's wedding at Temple Sha'arey Shalom in Springfield, 1981. Mildred Raphael was a convert to Judaism; two generations later, Jody Cohen, a rabbinical student at the time of her wedding, became a rabbi and currently occupies the position of southeastern regional director of Reform Judaism.

Vivienne Cohen

This is another photograph associated with a wedding—but of a very different sort. It shows the wedding in 1991 of Irving and Bella Chonowsky, the parents of the authors' dentist, Sid Chonowsky, who lives in Randolph and is pictured on the right. Irving and Bella, both Polish Jews, narrowly escaped the Nazis, having already lost almost their entire families. Bella, a resistance fighter in the Warsaw Ghetto, lost an eye when she was struck with a stick by a German soldier. Bella and Irving met in a Soviet labor camp in Omsk, Siberia, and fell in love. They were married "unofficially" in 1941 in the labor camp by a dying rabbi around whose bed they gathered for a brief ceremony. Their second wedding was organized by Sid and his sister Zina in conjunction with the celebration of their parents' fiftieth anniversary.
Sid Chonowsky

The overlap and interface of Jewish and American life is well illustrated in this July 15, 2000, photograph of Orthodox Jewish boy scouts from Troop 55 of Highland Park, at prayer in the synagogue-tent of Camp Kunatah, the only kosher boy scout camp in the United States. In the foreground is young Elon Weintraub, wearing his boy scout uniform complete with American flag while also wearing tefillin on his head and his arm. Jewish boy scouts can aspire to the Ner Tamid (Eternal Light) award, which makes one a kind of Jewish Eagle Scout.

Sheldon Freidenreich, scoutmaster of Troop 55

While liberal Jews generally oppose the display of religious symbols on public property as a violation of the church/state Establishment clause of the First Amendment, Orthodox Jews, especially Lubavitch Hasidim, have worked to celebrate Jewish symbols and holidays in public spaces. In this photograph, Governor Christie Whitman assists the leadership of the Rabbinical College of America (located in Morristown) in lighting a Chanukah lamp (chanukiah) in 1994. This annual tradition began during the administration of Governor Tom Kean and has continued during the administrations of Governors Jim Florio and Christie Whitman. Once lit, each lamp is hoisted via cherry picker atop a giant chanukiah in front of the State House in Trenton.

Rabbi Israel Teitelbaum, Rabbinical College of America, and the Office of the Governor of New Jersey

The lanterns for the second night of Chanukah have just been lit in Morristown's central square, the Green. The public celebration of the eight-night holiday has been repeated in Morristown for over two decades.
Rabbi Israel Teitelbaum, Rabbinical College of America

The Jewish Renaissance Fair, organized by the Rabbinical College of America and the Lubavitch Center of Essex County, is another sign of Jewish renewal. In 1998, the twentieth annual fair was held in Liberty State Park in Jersey City.
Rabbi Israel Teitelbaum, Rabbinical College of America

Jews gather to celebrate holidays but also to defend Jewish rights at home and abroad. Pictured are Jews from the Paterson area at a 1987 rally in Washington, D.C., for Soviet Jews.
Jewish Historical Society of North Jersey

MOSES BUSCH
MINSK 1868 - NEW BRUNSWICK 1929

LENA NACHMANOVICH BUSCH
MINSK 1872 – NEW BRUNSWICK 1946

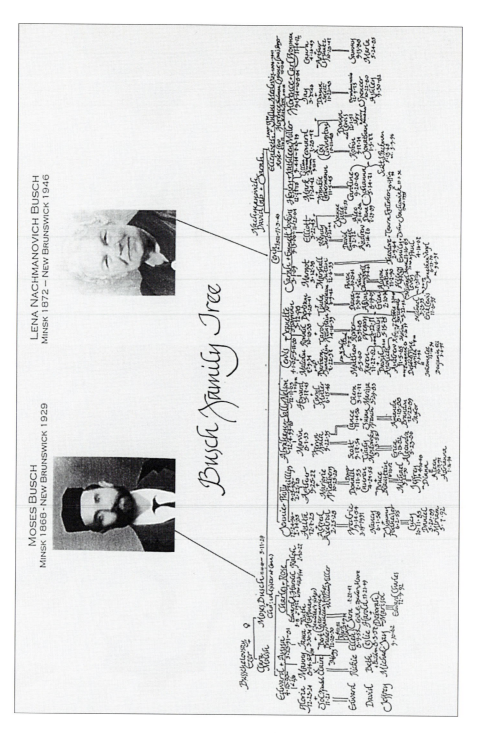

Busch Family Tree

The Busch family began its American sojourn in New Brunswick on John Street in 1904, but is now spread around New Jersey. As an example of how tied the family is to its history, it puts out a calendar from time to time that updates the family tree, provides an ongoing history of the family, lists birthdays, and even includes recipes. The family tree from the 1997 calendar is reproduced here. The progenitors of the family were Moses Busshlovsky (whose name became Busch in America) and Lena Nachmanovich, both of whom were born near Minsk in Russia.

Karen Anolick

The Buchbinders of New Jersey are another example of the power of Jewish family ties. Shown in this 1991 photo are some of the sixty family members who gathered to celebrate what would have been the one hundredth anniversary of the American founders of their family, Meyer and Emma Buchbinder, who were married in 1891 and settled in Bayonne, where they founded Buchbinder's Bakery. The members of the family pictured here sport T-shirts featuring Meyer and Emma at their wedding, shown in the photo below.
David L. Cowen

Meyer and Emma Buchbinder in the wedding photo that was reproduced on the T-shirts of their descendants. Meyer and Emma were never quite sure whence they had emigrated. Sometimes they would say "Poland," sometimes "Austria." They may actually have come from what became Czechoslovakia, which was between Poland and Austria and was not created until after World War I with the breakup of the Austro-Hungarian Empire. Jewish immigrants have often been uncertain of their country of origin because of shifting borders, especially in the Pale of Settlement to which they were confined. This has occasioned a standard Jewish joke. He: "It's settled. We live in Poland." She: "Thank God. Now I don't have to go through another Russian winter."
Flora Buchbinder Cowen

The continuity of family: David Cowen of Monroe Township, then ninety (pictured at far right in the back row of the Buchbinder family in the photo on page 147) walking with his great-grandson Zachary Jay, then eighteen months, of Marlboro, in 1999.
David L. Cowen

About the Authors

PATRICIA M. ARD is an assistant professor of English at Ramapo College of New Jersey. The author of numerous scholarly articles, she also edited and wrote the introduction to the reissue of Mary Peabody Mann's 1887 novel on African-Cuban slavery, *Juanita: A Romance of Real Life in Cuba Fifty Years Ago,* published by the University of Virginia Press (2000).

MICHAEL AARON ROCKLAND is a professor and the chair of the American Studies Department at Rutgers University. He is the author of eight books, including *The American Jewish Experience in Literature* (Haifa University Press, 1975). Three of his other books have been published by Rutgers University Press (*Homes on Wheels,* 1980; *Looking for America on the New Jersey Turnpike,* 1989; and *Snowshoeing Through Sewers,* 1994).

MOSES BUSCH
MINSK 1868 – NEW BRUNSWICK 1929

Busch Ja...

Busschelovsky, Ezer + ♀

Clara Molish — Moses Busch 12·4·68 ~ 3·11·29
Chd: cd (sister of Clara)

Edward + Anna 4·10·90~ / 3·23·91~01
- Gloria 12·23·24 + Joe Nankel 11·21
  - Edward
  - David
  - Jeffrey
- Manny 8·14·27/~99 × Claire "Maggy 12·28·30
  - Rickie
  - Beth
  - Michael Jay 9·10·62
- Irma 3·30·34 + Bert Bruder
  - Ellen 8·9·55 + Erik E. Bruder-Moore
  - Ceslie + children 8·3·5?

Charles + Rose
- Edward A. Harold 8·15 ~1922 w·1926 d·12/31/44
- Ralph 2·10·27
- Ruth Hoffman (Jeanette's sister) later married William Miller Jeanette's brother
  - Sara .7·27·47
  - Harold 11·21·49 Deborah) ~Marisol
    - Edward Charles 12·9·92

Jennie + Philip Phillips 12·24·96~ / 9·25·98~ 2·14·05 / 2·22·70
- Anita 12·7·25 + Alfred Axelrod 2·25·28
  - Fredric 9·14·54 / 3·19·1991
  - Nancy 6·1·56 + Jimmy Podheiser 6·2·55
    - Lucy 10·11·85
    - Daniel 5·20·09
    - Miriam 5·7·92
- Arthur 9·25·27 + Marjorie Friedberg 10·25·28
  - Donald 7·11·53 + Doyo
  - Lauren 4·24·56 + Bruce Blaustein 6·16·52
    - Michael 5·2·90
    - Jeffrey + 4·10·50 ~Diana
      - Alexa 10·15·92
      - Adrianna 1·16·96

Abraham + Sally Nel... 12·4·99~80 / 12·11~
- Marvin 8·1·33 + Irma Jack 9·22·35
  - Scott 9·17·54 + Cindy Moskowsky 3·3·55
    - Erica 7·13·82
    - Alexandra 5·23·06
  - Lance 11·14·56 + Susan French 3·29·...
    - Amanda 8·18·80
    - Brandon 12·22·09
    - Taylor
- Howard 5·17~ + Caryl M... 6·15~
  - Charles 3·17~
  - Marisa 3·29·...